Barry Silverberg, Director
Operating within the
Governmental and Community Relations Department
Austin Community College
Linda Young, Special Assistant to the President
5930 Middle Fiskville Rd., Austin, TX 78752
(512) 223-7076   bsilverb@austincc.edu
www.nonprofittexas.org

THE
COURAGE
TO
LEAD

AN ESSENTIAL GUIDE FOR
VOLUNTEER LEADERS, BOARD
TRUSTEES, AND PUBLIC SERVANTS

BY

ROBERT A. FLOYD

1st WORLD
LIBRARY
The World's Publisher

Austin, Texas

The Courage to Lead
By Robert A. Floyd

© Robert A. Floyd, 2003
The Courage to Lead

F&F Publishing
1st World Library
8015 Shoal Creek Blvd. Ste. 100
Austin, TX 78757
512-339-4000
www.1stworldlibrary.com

Library of Congress Control Number: 2003107179
ISBN: 0-9718562-7-3

First Edition

Senior Editor
Barbara Foley

Editing
Brad Fregger
Bob Mahoney

Book Design
Amelia Nottingham-Martin

Dedicated to the memory of my parents

Arthur H. (Red) Floyd

and

Olene Casbeer Floyd

Teachers

PREFACE

"Leadership is leaders acting — as well as caring, inspiring and persuading others to act — for certain shared goals that represent the values — the wants and needs, the aspirations and expectations — of themselves and the people they represent. And the genius of leadership lies in the manner in which leaders care about, visualize, and act on their own and their followers' values and motivations."

James MacGregor Burns

Sweat poured off me like Niagara Falls as I tried to stand straight with a 75-pound duffle bag draped over my shoulder. The drill sergeant barked at my fellow recruits and I knew my time was coming.

When it came my turn, the drill sergeant positioned his nose about one inch from mine and proceeded to shower me with his spittle. I don't remember what he asked me, nor my reply. He just stared into my eyes and said, "Bullsh**." A native Texan, I was not unfamiliar with the word, but never had I heard it enunciated with such clarity and intensity.

After what felt like a lifetime of his insulting my manhood he said, "When you get to Sgt. Jones, tell him you're the man."

I said, "Yes sir."

"Wrong, you lowly piece of sh**," he barked, "I am not a sir. I am a drill sergeant."

"Yes, drill sergeant." As he walked off to torment the next shaking recruit, I wondered about the seeming paradox of being "the man" as well as being just another "lowly piece of sh**."

Later, I found out being "the man" meant I had been designated as platoon leader for my basic training company. Having absolutely no idea what was expected of me, I knew only two things for certain on that sweltering day in 1968 at Ft. Bliss, Texas: First, I was going to Vietnam as sure as the wind blows in West Texas; second, for the next two months I would be a lowly piece of sh**.

Six weeks later, I found myself standing between two muscular members of my platoon, one with his army trunk lifted above his waist ready to heave it at his opponent, the other with his entrenching tool raised to smash his opponent's skull.

Stepping between them, I thought, "At least I won't die in Vietnam ... I will never leave Texas." As platoon leader, I had no real authority over these two angry young soldiers. I was just one buck private standing between two others, each of us wishing he were somewhere else.

Before either could strike the first blow, I had the presence to threaten them with the worst punishment a trainee could imagine. Not jail or a court marshal. Not a thousand pushups or a twenty-mile run.

I said, "If the drill sergeant comes in, you will be recycled back to day one of basic training."

Of all the fates trainees dreaded, this was the worst imaginable. You could almost see the testosterone draining from their bodies at the thought of having to start over.

After basic training, I never saw either guy again. I did go to Vietnam and have often wondered if they did and if they survived. I think of the incident as my first real test of leadership. While in the scheme of things it was infinitely insignificant, it provided a lesson that has stayed with me for over thirty years: *Leadership is not a rank or position. Leadership must always be earned.*

✦✦✦✦✦✦

I will never have the honor or privilege of knowing Todd Beamer and I seriously doubt he was thinking of himself as a leader when he boarded United Flight 93 on 9/11. A few short minutes later, Todd would answer the call. When he said "Let's roll," he had no way of knowing he would touch the hearts of so many Americans. Todd and his fellow passengers courageously overpowered the terrorists on United Flight 93, saving the lives of an untold number of their fellow citizens and earning the right to be immortalized as heroes in truest American heritage.

I do not know how Todd's leadership capacity developed, but I am certain of this: There was something in his character and past experiences which prepared him for that final terrible challenge. The passengers of United Flight 93 trusted Todd to be their leader in those last moments of their lives.

CONTENTS

ACKNOWLEDGEMENTS

Throughout my career, I have been blessed with many wonderful people in my life who have advised me, supported my efforts, and cared enough to help me succeed. By definition, the nonprofit, volunteer-management field is characterized by service, sharing, and unselfishness. I have found this to be true in each of my employing organizations and with those groups where I have served as a volunteer leader.

With trepidation I list the names of those to whom I owe much, knowing that aging brain cells may have unintentionally forgotten a good friend. If you are one of these, please accept my apology; I know this is probably just one more of many times you have indulged me.

I was fortunate to have had several Chief Elected Officers who were not only unselfish in their devotion to the organization, but went out of their way to befriend and nurture me. To each of you, my heartfelt appreciation:

The following chairmen of the board of the Texas Motor Transportation Association: Mike Craddock, K. L. Breeden, Terry Shope, Hardy McAlister, and Sam Bishop.

My four chairmen of the board during my four years as President and CEO of the Texas Society of Association Executives (TSAE): Bill Wolters, CAE, Texas Automobile Dealers Association; Brad Duggan, CAE, Just for the Kids; Bob Hale, CAE, Houston Association of Realtors; and Chris Williston, CAE, Independent Bankers Association of Texas

I have had the opportunity to serve as a fellow staff member with some of the most terrific people in the world. They were dedicated in giving of their talents and loyal support and in not hesitating to challenge me when I so often needed it. They are:

At the Texas Motor Transportation Association (TMTA): Barbara Lau; Cathy Brandewie; Eloise Carlisle; Jan Hughes; Jim Shillingburg, CAE; Jack Bryan (deceased); Kellyn Murray, CAE; Charles Dicker; Joann Cummings; Bill Duncan, CAE; Steve Parrino; Teresa Cage; John Danks, CAE; Tim Raven, CAE; and especially, Deborah Swift, friend, counselor, and the most creative person I have ever known.

At the Texas Society of Association Executives (TSAE): Jill Weir, CAE; D.J. Kyle, CAE; Linda LeFan; Linda Rudwick; Judy McDonald; Candy Minshew; and Rita Glover.

I'd also like to acknowledge fellow nonprofit and association executives and board members who served as role models: Linc Williston, CAE (deceased); George Allen, CAE; Richard Bettis, CAE; Bill Taylor, CAE; Jon Grove, CAE; John Kemp, CAE (deceased); Roy Vaughn, CAE; Walter Wainwright, CAE; Pam Heeman, CAE; Susan Sarfati, CAE; Barry Silverberg; and my predecessor at TSAE, Marilyn Monroe Bettis, CAE, who dedicated more than a quarter century of her life to TSAE and the association management profession.

My Publisher Brad Fregger, who encouraged and cajoled when appropriate, and to my editors, Barbara Foley and Bob Mahoney who did the final polishing.

Thanks to Tom Clowe, Ron Kessler, Bob Lively, Jim Nugent, Greg Maksymowicz, and Hank Erkel whose mentorship and friendship helped me maintain self-respect and self-confidence through a dark period in my life.

To the Honorable James E. Taylor, CAE, (deceased): military hero, Texas State Senator, Certified Association Executive and mentor. There will never be another General Taylor.

Gene Fondren, CAE, President of the Texas Automobile Dealers Association; and Mickey Moore, retired president of the Texas Retailers Association: mentors, life-time friends and consummate association leaders, who advised me on too many occasions to remember.

And, there's Terry Townsend, CAE, retired President of the Texas Hospital Association and Texas Motor Transportation Association. From the day Terry hired me in June, 1973, to his most recent telephone call, he has been my mentor, friend, encourager and cheerleader. He never told me no and will always be the definitive servant leader.

Kimberly Floyd Ferguson and Leslie Floyd, our daughters, two delightful, independent, young women. Fortunately, they inherited more of their mother's genes than mine.

And last but never least, Sherry Floyd, my beautiful wife and childhood sweetheart, the wind beneath my wings, whose judgment regarding men is surely questioned by all who know me.

Special Acknowledgement

If you have ever had need of someone whose love is totally unconditional, get a golden retriever—maybe two. Henry and Waylon were literally by my side during the writing of this book. They were not always helpful, however, as when sticking their noses under my wrist, knocking my hand from the mouse, and sending the cursor into the twilight zone. Maybe it was intentional. Maybe it helped.

FOREWORD

by Barry Silverberg

Martin Luther King proclaimed in the 1960s: "It may be that the greatest tragedy of this period of social transition is not the blaring noisiness of the so-called bad people, but the appalling silence of the so-called good people."

Silence is a crime as well as a tragedy in a time like ours when the lack of or failure of leadership resonates in every sector of our society. With so many opportunities for individuals to exercise leadership, we instead experience ever-increasing numbers retreating from leadership. Even worse, the ranks of the apathetic and wantonly critical grow and are rewarded by the public cynicism that is so pervasive in our time.

As Robert Floyd eloquently proves, leadership is attitudinal. It is not positional. It is neither accrued nor exercised only by virtue of being elected, appointed, or promoted.

Leadership takes root based on our personal credibility and derives from the essence of who we each are as sacred beings. It is a mantle that can be assumed by anyone and everyone, regardless of race, religion, nationality, gender, or socioeconomic status.

Leadership can be displayed and exercised by anyone with the courage to lead. That courage derives from a sense of self, personal integrity, and the willingness to take whatever risks may be necessary to be true to one's values and principles.

Eli Wiesel relates a midrash (Jewish teaching story) that encapsulates an important dimension of the courage to lead:

One of the Just Men came to Sodom determined to save its inhabitants from sin and punishment. Night and day he walked the streets and markets preaching against greed and theft, falsehood and indifference. In the beginning, people listened and smiled ironically. Then, they stopped listening: he no longer even amused them. Killers went on killing, the wise kept silent, as if there were no Just Man in their midst.

One day a child, moved by compassion for the unfortunate preacher, approached him with these words: "Poor stranger. You shout, you expend yourself body and soul; don't you see that it is hopeless?"

"Yes, I see," answered the Just Man.

"Then why do you go on?"

"I'll tell you why. In the beginning, I thought I could change man. Today I know I cannot. If I still shout today, if I still scream, it is to prevent man from ultimately changing me."

Is there a more important reason for leaders to heed the words of Martin Luther King and not be among the silent?

Regrettably, the nonprofit (third) sector holds no advantage over the government (first) and business (second) sectors when it comes to the scarcity of credible leaders with that all-important courage to lead. Too many huddle in hypocrisy and allow our sector to fail to reach our unparalleled potential to do good for so many. The failure to be credible leaders pervades our nonprofit sector.

It is extraordinarily refreshing and motivating to read each section of Robert Floyd's *The Courage to Lead*. His organization of this book defines leadership.

I had the honor of publishing Robert Floyd's first version of the chapter on "Inspiration". At the time, I was only beginning to know Robert, having begun our relationship as he relates in the chapter on "Passion."

The piece was published in the journal I was then producing, *Beyneynu* (Hebrew for "between you, me, and the gatepost"). I was stunned then and remain awed today by the story's simple eloquence and profound reach.

Robert closes that chapter about a man who shines shoes for his living by stating, "Leadership is not a place, but it can be found in unexpected places. In the Grand Hyatt Washington, I found not only a leader who literally shines, but also an example of shining leadership."

As you explore this wisdom-filled volume, I know that you will join me in reflecting on how something similar might be said of its author.

Indeed, resting in your hands is a compilation of time-less wisdom, bringing to mind the teachings of Lao Tzu, the Chinese philosopher, who wrote in his *Tao Te Ching* (as translated in John Heider's *The Tao of Leadership*):

> If your life works you influence your family.
>
> If your family works, your family influences the community.
>
> If your community works, your community influences the nation.
>
> If your nation works, your nation influences the world.
>
> If your world works, the ripple effect spreads throughout the cosmos.

In *The Courage to Lead*, Robert Floyd has captured the essence of what it means to lead, and to be a leader. May his ripple effect spread throughout the cosmos.

B'Shalom (In peace),

Barry Silverberg
Director, Center for Community-Based & Nonprofit Organizations at Austin Community College (Austin, Texas)
www.nonprofitaustin.org
11 September 2003

INTRODUCTION

Why This Book?

> *"These are the hard times in which a genius would wish to live ... Great necessity calls forth great leaders."*
>
> –Abigail Adams to Thomas Jefferson

After almost 30 years of working for, serving on, and consulting with nonprofit and public-sector boards of directors, I have reached the following conclusions.

- The overwhelming majority of board members, volunteer or elected, have the best interests of the organization/community at heart; and each is committed to doing the best job possible to achieve the mission, solve the problems, and accomplish the goals of their constituents. Only a small minority seek board service to fulfill some personal agenda.

- Although volunteer-based organizations from both the nonprofit sector and the public sector have different missions, governance structures, and methods of selection or election; their boards of directors have very much in common. Whether a nonprofit philanthropic or a business trade association, a publicly elected school board, or a church board of deacons; the fundamental issues of effective governance, constituent accountability, financial stewardship, servant leadership, board-staff relationships, and responsibility for results are common to all.

- Board members bring a passion to the cause they are serving.

- While board members bring varied abilities to board service, leadership skills are often the most lacking.

- Even if individuals have solid leadership credentials, this is not a guarantee that as a collective board they will be effective.

- For whatever reasons, most boards are ambivalent, "too busy," or just plainly unaware their effectiveness could be increased tenfold by increasing their individual and collective leadership capacities.

- Boards generally are not proactive, nor do they pay enough attention to planning and to how change is affecting the organization and its constituents.

- It is an honor to serve on a nonprofit or public-sector board of directors and the vast majority of board members serve honorably.

✦✦✦✦✦✦

I first became actively interested in the subject of leadership in my late 30s when I decided my career goal was to be the CEO of a trade association. In 1973 I joined the Texas Motor Transportation Association (TMTA), a trade association representing the Texas trucking industry, and after 10 years of service, I knew with certainty this was the career path for me.

At about the same time, I was selected to participate in Leadership Austin, an organization sponsored by the Greater Austin Chamber of Commerce. The mission of Leadership Austin is to provide leadership training for potential young leaders and to encourage them to become involved in community-service activities.

Motivated by this experience, I ran for the school board in the Eanes (Austin, Texas) Independent School District, where our oldest daughter was enrolled. I was elected in 1982 and re-elected in 1985.

My school-board service was my first real experience at serving on a board of directors, although I had served briefly as an elected member of a small water-utility district. Serving on the school board coincided with my growing desire to enhance my own leadership skills, so I began in earnest a lifelong study of leadership.

In the late 1980s, I became president of TMTA after my mentor and friend, Terry Townsend, resigned to become CEO of a financial institution. I then had the opportunity to directly interact with our board of directors and become not only a participant but also an observer of the dynamics of volunteer boards.

Over the years, I have served in various capacities on boards of directors, including being Chair of the Texas Society of Association Executives (TSAE), an officer of the American Society of Association Executives (ASAE), the Mental Health in Texas Association, the Austin Convention and Tourism Bureau, and the Texas Association of Nonprofit Organizations (TANO).

My purpose for writing this book is to offer dedicated individuals some thoughts for increasing their own individual leadership skills, and suggest collective skills for a board working together to achieve their organization's mission.

Who Is My Intended Audience

This book had been germinating in the rocky soil of my mind for over a year when the attack on America occurred on September 11, 2001, and shortly thereafter the Enron Scandal hit the front page. I wrote a brief piece for a newsletter asking, "Where was the Enron board of directors?" Whether it was their own greed, ignorance, or duplicity, the Enron board had no valid excuses for allowing such shenanigans to happen on their watch. They were individually AWOL and collectively guilty of gross dereliction of duty.

Certainly the boards of for-profit corporations are different from nonprofit or public-sector boards; paid versus no pay is one major distinction. But when it comes to accountability, stewardship, responsibility, and servant leadership, the two types of boards share a strong family resemblance.

The vast majority of board members, both corporate and nonprofit, are good stewards, motivated by doing what is best for their constituents. But the one recurring weakness I have observed in boards is: While most understand their legal, financial, and oversight responsibilities, few have received any significant training in leadership.

For this reason, this book was written primarily for the dedicated leaders serving on boards of directors—or desiring to serve—who want to improve their skills and develop greater leadership capacity:

- Nonprofit organizations
- Trade associations
- Hospital boards of directors
- Churches and religious organizations
- Agricultural cooperatives
- Chambers of Commerce

- Public-sector boards
  - Elected
  - Appointed
- Other volunteer organizations

In addition, anyone who dedicates his or her service to a volunteer-based organization, whether paid staff, committee chair, donor, or in another volunteer capacity, can benefit from the principles of leadership offered in this book.

Hopefully, corporate boards will also find value in these pages.

How Did I Write This Book?

For this book, I relied on four principal resources:

- My own experience in leadership roles, as an association executive, a consultant, and as a member of various nonprofit and public-sector boards of directors
- Interviews with former colleagues and individuals, some of whom served as CEOs of nonprofit organizations or trade associations, some as board members, and some who served in both capacities
- I have drawn on the wisdom of some of the best leadership writers and practitioners to help readers assess their own leadership skills, strengths, and weaknesses. The writing and research of these outstanding authors have been major influences on my professional leadership development.
- Autobiographies and biographies of exceptional leaders

How To Use This Book

If you visit your local bookstore or library, you can find literally hundreds of titles that contain the word *leadership*. In fact, my wife suggested that I title this book: ***The Courage to Lead: Not Just another DAMN Book on Leadership***.

I plead guilty. This is "another DAMN Book on Leadership," and I know from experience the best leaders are incredibly busy people. You don't have the time, even if you have the motivation, to spend hours reading. I frankly do not know if there are *21 Steps to Great Leadership, The 10 Essential Qualities of Effective Leaders, or The 15 Absolutely Unassailable, Never-to-Be-Challenged Attributes of a Successful Leader.*

So please use this book however it will be the most helpful to you. Each chapter is a stand-alone essay. Read it from end to end or choose those chapters that have the most immediate appeal. **And most importantly, you are hereby given total immunity from feeling guilty if you don't read every word. My purpose is to enlighten, not to add to your burdens.**

AUTHENTICITY

"The first person to lead is you. We earn the right to lead others when they see us lead well in our own lives."
–John Maxwell

"I cannot consent to place in the control of others one who cannot control himself."
–General Robert E. Lee

"An authentic leader not only speaks the truth, but lives the truth"
–Robert A. Floyd

<u>9/11/2001</u>: Captain Frances Callahan, a 30-year veteran of the New York Fire Department, died leading his men at the World Trade Center. He was eulogized by a fellow captain:

"Firefighters and their officers share a... special relationship. Officers very literally lead firefighters into harm's way."

(12/01/01: Enron Corporation files for bankruptcy and announces 4,000 layoffs.)

Captain Callahan's Eulogy: *"We go first. If things go badly, we are required by our oath and tradition to be the last of our command to leave."*

(Enron executives sold $924 million worth of company shares in 2000 and 2001.)

Back to the Eulogy: *"Accountability for our men is carved into our heart. Responsibility for our men, their wives and children are in the depth of our soul."*

(December 2001. Enron employees lose up to 90 percent of their 401(k) retirement savings.)

The Eulogy: *"Camaraderie is sharing hardship. It's lungs that burn from exertion ... it's not to be asleep on your watch. It is trust, it is responsibility, it is acting honorably."*

(12/12/01. Enron CEO Ken Lay refuses to attend Congressional hearing. U.S. Senate to subpoena Enron papers.)

The Eulogy: *"Captain Frank Callahan did not fail in his leadership ... He lead his command ... he was the last to leave. If more of our world's leaders were forged as he was, ours would be a better world."*

Authentic Leadership: You choose between Captain Francis Callahan of the NYPD and Kenneth Lay of Enron. Captain Callahan and his comrades literally ran through fire to save others, with no regard for their own safety. With total disregard for others, Kenneth Lay and other corporate con-men ran through excuses like allergy sufferers through *Claritin*.

✦✦✦✦✦✦✦

Authenticity begins with self-awareness. After making the unwavering commitment to being the best leader possible, you must honestly assess your own strengths and weaknesses as a leader. "Know Thyself." The willingness to engage in thoughtful introspection and honest self-appraisal is at the center of every successful leader.

This does not require major psychoanalysis, but a clear and honest understanding of your own strengths and weaknesses. If you don't know your own shortcomings, you can be certain everyone else will. By understanding and acknowledging both your pluses and minuses, you will gain confidence as you build on your strong points and minimize your weaker areas.

Author Peter Drucker writes, "Effective executives build on their strengths ... on what they can do. They do not build on weakness. They do not start out with things they cannot do." So if you start your volunteer service by knowing your own strengths and weaknesses, you can learn to build on your strengths and be a more effective volunteer leader.

In an international study of chief executive officers from 28 countries, Robert Rosen and his research team identified "personal literacy" as a prerequisite for leaders of major global corporations. Their findings relate directly to leaders on nonprofit and community boards. " Personal literacy involves understanding and valuing yourself. *Leaders must be self-aware, open, honest, and committed to their own learning.*" (my emphasis)

I am an ardent admirer of Frances Hesselbein, currently the president and CEO of The Drucker Foundation and the former chief executive of the Girl Scouts of America. Ms. Hesselbein, herself an authentic leader, has noted eight personal barriers to effective leadership:

1. A lack of formal, articulated personal goals, written and close at hand, and a road map of how to meet them

2. No clear understanding of one's own strengths and weaknesses, plus a plan for improving

3. Not understanding there is only one standard for ethics in both our personal and professional lives

4. A lack of generosity, not sharing time, ideas, feedback, and compliments with others

5. Leading from the rear, sitting on the fence, and never taking responsibility

6. Always stressing what others can't do well rather than building on what they can do well

7. Playing "Chicken Little" instead of "The Little Engine That Could." Lack of a positive approach to serious issues and failing to suggest reasonable solutions

8. Not taking charge of one's own personal learning and development

A leader who takes personal responsibility for their own actions and shares what they know with others is practicing role-modeling at its best. By their willingness to confront their own shortcomings, they give courage to others to be honest with themselves.

With authentic leaders, what you see is what you get. They do not change their stripes; they build their reputation and trust by being consistent in their actions and by treating each person with dignity. They may change their minds, strategies, and even attitudes toward certain situations and circumstances, but their character is constant.

An authentic leader never lies to himself or about himself. As Warren Bennis notes, "We are our own raw material. ... Only when we know what we're made of and what we want to make of it can we begin our lives. ... The leader cannot cut his conscience to fit this year's fashions."

Authentic leaders are dependable. Followers know that a leader who has always tried to do the right thing can be depended upon to do what he thinks is right. We may disagree with his position or decision, but seldom with his motives.

General Colin Powell is an authentic leader. As a person of color, General Powell has faced discrimination all his life, including his early military years as an aspiring career officer.

He rose to be the nation's highest ranking military officer, not by rejecting his rich culture and heritage, but by continuing to embrace it at the same time he was embracing the principles and tradition of the United States Army. The officers and enlisted men and women under his various commands knew he had their best interests uppermost in his mind every day.

General Powell acts consistently with his own professional and personal values. In his leadership role as U.S. Secretary of State he often has to roll with the punches, and as a good soldier, must sometimes carry out orders of his Commander-in-Chief that he disagrees with.

However, I have little doubt that if he were ever asked to violate his principles or core beliefs, he would resign his appointment immediately. Whether leading the most powerful military in the world, serving as the country's top diplomat, or working tirelessly to help young people through *America's Promise: The Alliance for America's Youth*, General Powell has proven time and time again that he walks his talk.

✦✦✦✦✦✦✦

Interestingly, the words "authenticity" and "authority" have in common their first four and last three letters; yet they bear precious little resemblance to one another in the context of leadership. Having authority—as various corporate executives and religious officials have demonstrated—is not synonymous with leadership.

A clear distinction between authentic leaders and authoritarians is their attitude toward promises. Authentic leaders keep promises and expect others to do the same. Those who think their authority gives them carte blanche

over their own behavior while expecting others to pay
homage are deluding no one but themselves.

The former Boston archbishop, Cardinal Bernard Law,
was finally forced to resign under mounting fire for his
mishandling of sexual-abuse issues in his archdiocese. For
several months, Cardinal Law arrogantly displayed an attitude that he was, pardon the pun, above the law. His total
downfall might have been mitigated had he chosen to accept
responsibility for his mistakes and mismanagement.

"Character is destiny," wrote Heraclitus. A leader of a
volunteer or community-based organization must have an
impeccable character as they have been chosen to have the
best interests of their peers at heart. While no leader is
without flaws, an effective leader knows their own and works
hard to overcome them.

++++++

Authentic leaders are accountable to their followers,
their superiors, and their stakeholders. "Accountability,"
writes Jean Lipman-Blumen, "means the leader knows
beforehand that every choice will be seriously scrutinized.
Accountability, coupled with authenticity, blocks unethical,
irresponsible, or simply thoughtless action ... constituents
expect full disclosure."

Barely into his Presidency, John F. Kennedy displayed
the accountability and responsibility that made him a war
hero when his PT Boat 109 collided with a Japanese
destroyer off the Solomon Islands on August 2, 1943. After
his boat was cut in half, Kennedy towed a wounded sailor to
safety by holding on to a strap of his life vest with his teeth
for four heroic hours. Kennedy and several of his crew were
stranded for six days before they were rescued.

In April, 1961, Kennedy gave the order to proceed
with what became a notorious military disaster and major
embarrassment to the United States. The infamous attack

on Cuba at the Bay of Pigs was a total failure and the exiled invaders were routed, killed, or captured within three days. The attack, which was intended to overthrow the Castro government, failed because of poor intelligence, a flawed strategy, and inadequate resources.

Kennedy went on national television and took complete responsibility for the disaster; he did not try to pass the buck to U.S. intelligence sources or to the ill-fitted commanders. As a leader, he understood that it was his unconditional responsibility and his alone.

Following his speech, a national public opinion poll found Kennedy's approval rating had risen to 61 percent. Americans were not approving of his actions but were applauding his willingness to admit he had made a mistake and to take full responsibility for his actions. Kennedy knew accountability could not be delegated.

✦✦✦✦✦✦✦

In any organization, the board of directors has the most powerful role and they are charged with the most accountability. Individual members are accountable to each other as well as to the board itself. They are also accountable to those who selected them to lead and serve.

To borrow a reference from the corporate world, leaders must be accountable to their stockholders, not their own stock options; to their people, not their own pocketbooks. Leaders of nonprofit and community-based organizations are no less accountable to their constituents than if they were drawing seven-figure salaries.

CHANGE

"Great Souls have always met with violent opposition from mediocre minds."
                                            –Albert Einstein

"He who will not apply new remedies must expect new evils; for time is the greatest innovator."
                                            –Francis Bacon

"If we don't change our direction, we'll end up exactly where we are headed."
                                            –Ancient Chinese Proverb

"The leader as Change Agent is the driving force for positive change in the organization."

New York Times, Dateline: Washington, D.C., April 29, 2002: "About 20 American soldiers flew to the former Soviet republic of Georgia today, the first of 150 to 200 Special Forces G.I.s who will train and equip army, border and security personnel there, the Pentagon said."

American soldiers training former Soviet military personnel? Do you think former Soviet Premier Nikita Khrushchev ever imagined this when he was pounding his table at the United Nations and telling America, "We will bury you."?

In the spring of 2000, I accompanied several other business executives on a tour of U.S. National Guard deployments in Europe. In a factory near Ramstein Air Force Base,

Germany, we observed National Guard personnel repairing
motors and transmissions on army vehicles, some of which
had been damaged in Bosnia.

American soldiers repairing U.S. Army vehicles in
Europe? No big deal, except in World War II, the same plant
was being used by the Nazis to build Panzer tanks to kill
American and Allied soldiers.

"The Times They Are a Changin" Bob Dylan sang in
the 60s, but as clairvoyant as Bob may have been, he couldn't
have anticipated the depth of change the world has seen in
the last years of the 20th Century and the beginning of the
21st. Words such as "unprecedented," "monumental," and
"whitewater," have been some of the favorites to describe our
changing environment. The best description may well be
this: "Making a deep change," writes Robert E. Quinn "is like
walking around naked into the land of uncertainty."

Of all the books published about change, my favorite is
The Change Monster by Jeanie Daniel Duck. What could be
more appropriate since we spend much of our time trying to
"duck" from the change monsters in our lives? But effective
leaders know they cannot "duck" change; they must be the
change leaders in their organizations and communities.
And, if you have not already learned, leading change is a lot
like riding a bucking bronco; you not only have to ride the
full eight seconds, but look good doing it.

The only person who likes change, it has been said, is a
wet baby. I worked 21 years for an organization filled with
some of the best people in the world. But they were as
resistant to change as I am to steamed broccoli. And when
change did come in the form of deregulation of their
industry, many were totally unprepared and paid a high
emotional and economic price.

Change seldom comes well-cushioned, which is all the
more reason for leaders of nonprofit organizations to plan,
prepare, and produce constructive change. In *Leading
Change: The Argument for Values-Based Leadership*,

author Jim O' Toole writes, "The task of a leader is to bring about that change in a way that is responsible to the true and long-term needs of all constituencies."

✦✦✦✦✦✦✦

"Begin with the end in mind," Dr. Stephen Covey advises. This is excellent advice when the organization begins a major change initiative. A clear objective is imperative, but no guarantee that you will reach your destination on time or without bruises. Be prepared for detours, and then more detours, along the bumpy road to change.

One bit of humorous advice before you begin your trip. If you want to prepare for the ups and downs of change, your board should buy some popcorn and rent the movie, *Vacation*. Just sit back and watch the Clark W. Griswolds struggle from their home in Chicago to the WallyWorld theme park in California.

During the two-week ordeal across the country, if anything can go wrong, it does. From taking a wrong turn into a not-so-nice part of St. Louis, where the family is fortunate to lose only their hubcaps, to Clark's final act of desperation when he finds WallyWorld closed, the Griswolds' trip is the ultimate metaphor for a strategic change initiative.

✦✦✦✦✦✦✦

Leading change is not for the fainthearted; as Machiavelli wrote, "Change has no constituency." Yet leading change may well be the most critical task a board of directors performs during its tenure. To lead change in your organization requires you to initially take three steps:

1. Focus on change as an opportunity, not a threat.

2. Assure yourself there is a compelling reason for the change, which can lead to major innovation in the organization.

3. Recognize from the beginning that you cannot "manage change;" by definition, change is unpredictable and often messy. You can, however, manage the process, but not without the help of others, patience, courage, endurance, and at least one case of Maalox.

In the wonderfully funny movie, *My Big Fat Greek Wedding*, the father of the bride-to-be is traditional Greek to his core. His worldview is: There are Greeks, and then there's everyone else. His work, family, and social life are centered on his extended Greek family.

His greatest despair is that his 30-year-old daughter has not yet married. But his despair turns to desperation when she falls in love with a non-Greek. Dad finally sees he is powerless to end the relationship. Finally with the relentless prodding of his wife and family members, he reluctantly begins to accept his fate—to have a non-Greek son-in-law.

He finally concedes if he can't change the couple's minds, he can at least have some say in the final outcome. He does this by presenting the bride and groom with a deed to a home as their wedding present. The last scene in the movie reveals that the house is next door to his!

✦ ✦ ✦ ✦ ✦ ✦ ✦

Peter Drucker writes, "Innovative organizations systematically look both outside and inside for clues to innovative opportunities. ... Refocus and change the organization when you are successful. When everybody else says, 'Don't rock the boat. If it ain't broke, don't fix it.' ... let's hope you have someone who is willing to be unpopular by saying, 'Let's improve it.' If you don't improve it, you go downhill pretty fast."

As association executive Pam Heeman, CAE, who runs a successful association-management company says, from the very moment the change initiative is verbalized, you have to be up-front with everyone that things are going to be different.

"Those most directly affected will have an immediate sense of loss and you must not hesitate to acknowledge the personal feelings and be prepared to discuss with all the clarity you can muster what you see as the outcome of the initiative."

Why do people in organizations resist change? The following responses are typical:

- We don't understand the reason for it.
- We lack information.
- We don't perceive a need to change.
- We feel we have already changed.
- We don't see what it means for us.
- We don't see a clear direction.
- We fear the loss of power, prestige, money, status, friends, and work.
- We are reluctant to give up something that is comfort-able and familiar.
- We were not asked for input about change.
- We have been hurt or betrayed by previous changes.
- We fear we may not be able to learn enough to be successful.
- We are already overwhelmed.
- We fear a loss of control.

As a volunteer leader, you cannot command change. Success depends on persuading your peers to be "Change Champions," to join with you in the change process, on a potentially very steep, uphill climb. James O'Toole writes, "The major source of resistance to change is the all-too-human objection to having the will of others imposed on us ... Everybody resists change—particularly the people who have to do the most changing."

Futurists/authors David Pearce Snyder and Gregg Edwards write: "While people *frequently initiate changes in their lives ... in a very real sense, it is organizations that resist change, not people. ...* It is the collective nature of the decision-making process within organizations that makes them resistant to change, not merely because it is slow, but mainly because it often requires people to take actions ... that are not necessarily beneficial to them."

Nonprofit consultant and writer Douglas Eadie says the board should ask this question in considering making a compelling change initiative: "What should the organization do that's new and different and that isn't likely to be accomplished through business as usual?" And once consensus has been reached, he adds this cautionary note: "Strategic change initiatives should be *only* those you can realistically expect to carry out without stretching the association too thin." (emphasis mine)

Eadie's advice: Think chewable bites! The board must not break off so much that the organization can't chew without causing major disruptions in operations. The change process is difficult enough without diverting precious resources that may be needed in running the day-to-day operations of the shop.

✦✦✦✦✦✦✦

10 Steps for Leading Change

1. The change initiative should be compelling, yield significant benefits, and capitalize on strengths and opportunities.

2. Change is constant, unpredictable, and is always accelerating.

3. Leverage technology as a key tool for organization, coordination, communication, research, marketing, and public relations.

4. Expect to be surprised.

5. Everybody resists change—clarify, communicate, consult, set the course—but never conceal.

6. Change before you are forced to change—it is hard to make a clear decision with a gun pointed at your head.

7. Take risks—prudent risks.

8. Enlist "Change Champions" to help support the change initiative.

9. Each change initiative should have a
   • Clear target or outcome.
   • Strategic Action Plan.
   • Budget/management of resources.

10. Stay the course.

CHOICES, COMMITMENTS, AND COSTS

"Leadership cannot be exercised from a distance."
–James Kouzes and Barry Posner

A good friend once asked me to join the board of directors of a nonprofit organization; I said yes, and it was a big mistake. The organization's mission appealed to me, but after attending only one board meeting, I realized I had failed to heed my own internal warning signs.

Like the plumber whose faucets are always leaking, the nonprofit consultant joined a nonprofit board that was fundamentally dysfunctional. After attending three meetings, and serving on a subcommittee, I made a not-so-graceful exit.

While many American workers have good luck, good genes, or good connections to be able to work in a field of their choosing; in this elongated season of mergers, consolidations, bankruptcies, and corporate mismanagement, more often than not the choices are made by someone else.

But in our vocational pursuits and volunteer efforts, most of us do have the power to choose which causes, organizations,

or activities we give our time and energy to. While perfect
teeth, mortgages, and college tuition may limit our work
options, we usually choose where we want to make a personal
difference, whether in our community, special cause, or professional organization.

Nonetheless, before you race off to serve whatever
worthy cause has your name on it, please proceed with
caution and reflection. If you are already giving of your time
and talents, it is still healthy to reflect on whether you are
being fulfilled or getting your fill of volunteering.

Show me a chamber of commerce, professional organization, or community group that has an abundance of great
volunteers and let's find a way to clone it. Most organizations
are constantly spending time and money trying to recruit a
new cadre of volunteers to replenish their dwindling supply
of people. Regrettably, many organizations do not do a good
job of recruiting, especially recruiting the right people to
serve in the right positions. This is what happened to me
when I agreed to serve on that nonprofit board without
doing my homework.

Too often, organizations recruit enthusiastic people,
but do not do their due diligence to see if they have the right
person for the right job. When this occurs, burnout can
happen, volunteer morale goes south, and the organization
can pay a heavy price in future recruitment efforts.

So look before you leap, particularly if you are being
recruited or nominated to serve in a leadership position in
the organization. You may have been the most successful and
energetic PTA president in the history of the school, but you
may not be the right fit to serve on the school board.

Even if you've served in every capacity that your church
has asked you to, from Sunday school teacher to building
committee chairman, before you accept a leadership role as
Chairman of the Board of Deacons, make sure you are
making a conscious choice based on self-evaluation and

quiet reflection; don't let yourself be railroaded by well-meaning friends.

Your choice of leadership roles should be based on what was first discussed in *Authenticity*—self-awareness. What are your strengths and weaknesses? What are your core values? What motivates you? Where do you want to have impact? Does the leadership commitment you are preparing to make fit your expertise, personal vision, and passion?

"Typically, when we consider a new position or role, we think about all the benefits," writes Sara King, the group director of the Center for Creative Leadership's Individual Leader Development. "Yet many times the costs are surprises; unforeseen aspects of our decision."

King offers the following "cost-benefit" analysis to help you determine if you are taking the oath to an office that will meet or exceed your own expectations and help you achieve your God-given potential.

Potential Benefits

- Pride of accomplishment
- Emotional rewards
- Self-validation
- Impact on people and events
- Service to others
- Meaning
- Attention and recognition
- Personal prominence
- New connections and acquaintances
- Helping others grow
- Personal status
- Singular achievements
- Heightened experiences
- Travel & education

Potential Costs

- Physical energy
- Long hours
- Too many meetings
- Constant obligations
- Responsibility
- Care-taking
- Less time for nonleadership work interests
- Visibility ("fishbowl")
- Public duties
- Isolation from peers
- Less freedom of expression
- Pressure to produce
- Stress on family
- Less time for family

COURAGE

"Courage is the first of human qualities because it is the quality which guarantees all others."
                                              –Winston Churchill

"Let's Roll!"
                        –Todd Beamer – Flight 93 – 9/11/01

"Courage is that quality in a leader that knows the difference between right and wrong and possesses the depth of character to act on that difference."
                                              –Robert A. Floyd

On Thursday, December 1, 1955, an African-American seamstress boarded a city bus in Montgomery, Alabama and sat with three other blacks in the fifth row, the first row that blacks could occupy. A few stops later, the front four rows were filled with whites, and one white man was left standing.

According to state law, blacks and whites could not occupy the same row, so the bus driver asked all four of the blacks seated in the fifth row to move. Three complied, but Rosa Parks refused. She was arrested.

Rosa Parks was not a "simple seamstress" as some accounts of the Montgomery Bus Boycott have told; she had been a long time worker in the National Association for the Advancement of Colored People (NAACP). Her refusal to give up her seat on that December day was no less an act of

incredible courage at a time when segregation was the way of
life in the South.

During the boycott, the Reverend Martin Luther King's
home was bombed and other members of the black community were threatened with physical intimidation and
violence. Black workers were told they no longer had jobs
and black farmers found their credit no longer good for
their crop loans.

Rosa Parks became a symbol for the Civil Rights
Movement, and finally the eyes of America focused on the
degradation and inhumanity of racism—and change came.
There would still be acts of violence and murder well into
the 1960s, but Rosa Parks and countless other unknown
heroes had sounded the trumpet. Slowly, but certainly, the
walls of segregation came tumbling down.

✦✦✦✦✦✦

When our thoughts turn to courage, we tend to focus
on great acts of bravery, such as the unselfish efforts on 9/11
of the passengers of Flight 93; Lance Armstrong's winning
five Tour de France bicycle races after refusing to give in to
cancer; or the American Flag being raised over Iwo Jima.

Courage is the willingness to take great risks for a cause
you believe in. But it is often much more, and sometimes
much less dramatic. As John Kennedy noted, "The courage
of life is often a less dramatic spectacle than the courage of a
final moment; but it is no less a magnificent mixture of
triumph and tragedy."

Courage is getting up in the morning day after day to
fight the traffic, deal with difficult people, and work long
hours to support your family. Courage is the young man at
the community college where I teach, struggling with every
step as his braced legs, slowly but steadily, move him forward
to my class ... where he makes an A+.

Courage is the willingness to keep an open mind, change your position, and vote your convictions even if it means risking the support or friendship of those who may have chosen you to represent their interests. As a leader on a board of directors, you may at some time find yourself at odds with public opinion as well as with friends and neighbors.

In the 1980s, the school board I served on was in a rapidly growing district and we were constantly searching for good sites to build new schools. Eventually our growth required us to build a new middle school and for the first time in our history, we had to establish boundary lines that divided the district.

If you have served on a school board, you are probably already nodding your head, knowing what's coming. Many parents were concerned that the new school would be inferior educationally or more importantly, wouldn't have the "prestige" of the long-time middle school. Emotions were high—rationality did not apply.

The school cafeteria was packed the night we were to vote on the boundaries. Many of our friends, opposed to the change, were sitting in the front row, daring us to vote in favor. One constituent, a former state supreme court justice, got a huge round of applause when he argued we should put such important matters to the patrons to vote on.

In one of my finer moments, I responded that we were elected to make difficult decisions and asked him why, while on the Supreme Court, he didn't submit his tough decisions to the voters of Texas? *Touché.* In the end, the board voted six to one to create the new boundaries. One mom came up to me and said, "Well, it's done; let's make the best of it."

And we did. The new school has been an overwhelming success educationally, athletically, and with outstanding parental support. On the scale of courageous acts, our decision barely registers. Fortunately most of us will never be faced with the kind of decision that Rosa Parks or Todd Beamer and his fellow passengers had to make.

When you take the oath of office for a nonprofit board, city council, or school board, you must be prepared to make an unpopular decision because you believe it to be the right decision. It's part of the territory and you will find that the sun still rises.

++++++

Courage is that quality of leadership that sustains the leader when there are two setbacks for every step forward. Courage is when you are being hammered relentlessly by the waves of change or discontent, but refuse to allow your convictions to be swept away by the tide. Courage is not losing your perspective even though the pressure is constant.

John F. Kennedy called courage "the most admirable of human virtues," and frequently referred to it as "grace under pressure," as Ernest Hemmingway defined it. President Kennedy wrote in his book, *Profiles in Courage*, about eight United States senators who had the courage of their convictions to overcome "the unpopularity of their courses, the defamation of their characters, and sometimes, but sadly only sometimes, the vindications of their reputations and their principles."

Kennedy himself exhibited grace under pressure many times, from his days as a hero in World War II to the handling of the Cuban Missile Crisis during thirteen days in October, 1962. Leadership skills may not be as necessary when times are good; it is during the times of adversity when the mantle of leadership is tested and skills are honed to an art.

Terry Townsend, who served as Chairman of The Board of the American Society of Association Executives (ASAE) in 1981-82, recalls an incident when the CEO and top leadership wanted to change the fundamental structure of ASAE from an individual to a corporate-based membership. Most of the leadership was backing the CEO, but not all of the membership supported this radical change.

At the annual convention, one member of the board, Rod Geer, at great risk to his own professional advancement in ASAE, debated the CEO on the issue. Rod did such a wonderful job of presenting the case for remaining a professional membership society that the membership overwhelmingly rejected the proposal to change.

And like John Kennedy's eight senators, Rod paid the price by being blackballed for several years from moving up in the chairs of ASAE. Yet if a person has the courage of his convictions, he never has to look back and wish he had remained silent.

Happily, this story had a good ending. Ultimately, Rod became the ASAE Chair. He was a man, in John Kennedy's words, whose "need to maintain his own respect for himself was more important to him than his popularity with others—because his conscience, his personal standards of ethics, his integrity ... were stronger than the pressures of public disapproval—because his faith that his course ... would ultimately be vindicated ... "

✦✦✦✦✦✦

"To have courage," writes author Peter Koestenbaum, "is to think for yourself. It is to reason independently when assaulted with conflicting opinions. It is to be clear and have firm values, of which you are proud and support under stress. It is to have faith—in yourself, your family, your organization, your religion, your country, your profession, your organization, your friends."

With television cameras pointed at her like massed artillery, Sherron Watkins raised her hand to "tell the whole truth and nothing but the truth." Standing before a committee of the Congress of the United States, Watkins, the former vice president for corporate development for Enron Corporation, testified on Valentine's Day, 2002, that she had warned former Enron CEO Kenneth Lay in a seven-page memo that she was worried that "we will implode in a wave of accounting scandals." Members of Congress later praised her integrity and courage in exposing the corporate irresponsibility of Enron's top management.

In the fifth grade, Colleen Rowley set a goal to join the Federal Bureau of Investigation the moment she became eligible, a goal she realized. A scant three months after Sherron Watkins' testimony, Special Agent Rowley was also before the Congress testifying about a memo that she had sent to her boss, FBI Director Robert Mueller: "To get to the point, I have deep concerns that a delicate and subtle shading/skewing of facts by you and others at the highest levels of FBI management has occurred and is occurring." The memo was referring to the FBI investigation in the aftermath of 9/11.

Cynthia Cooper returned to her hometown of Clinton, Mississippi, in 1991, and later became the head of the internal audit team of WorldCom. Told by a senior official to "back off," she persisted against great odds to reveal the illegal accounting practices that brought down the giant telecom company. Shortly after Cooper broke the news to the audit committee of the WorldCom board, the senior official was fired and later indicted on security fraud charges.

Watkins, Rowley, and Cooper independently expressed a combination of anger and indignation about actions taken by their superiors. They told of ignored warnings, midnight shredding, bureaucratic buffoonery, and as we know now, criminal conduct.

In the popular lexicon of exposing government or corporate shenanigans, all three of these women were "blowing the whistle" on behavior they believed to be detrimental to their organizations and just plain wrong. Although "whistle-blower" is defined in the American Heritage Dictionary as "one who reveals wrongdoing within an organization to the public or to those in positions of authority," whistle-blowing often conjures up a negative image, like "tattletale" in elementary school.

In his most recent book, *Crossing the Unknown Sea: Work as a Pilgrimage of Identity*, David Whyte tells the story of his waking in the middle of the night and realizing that his boat was drifting perilously close to the rocks in the choppy waters off the Galapagos Islands. He awakened just in time to steer the boat away from the rocks and avoid what could have been a fatal encounter for the ship's crew.

The captain of the ship was new and had fallen asleep. But later as his initial anger at the captain began to slip away, Whyte realized it was too convenient to place all the blame at the captain's feet.

The ship's previous captain was "a robust, strapping man ... and the great irony of his all-knowing alertness," was that he had lulled Whyte and the other crew members "*into a lack of responsibility at the very core.*"

Later Whyte told the story of the near-disaster to a recently retired admiral from the U.S. Navy. The admiral summed it all up: "A good crew doesn't let a new captain fail." Nor, of course, does a worthy captain fail his crew.

Lay of Enron ran away from his responsibility with all the speed of a wildebeest escaping the jaws of the hungry lion, while his crew ran their corporate ship aground.

In Whyte's imagery, Rowley, Watkins, and Cooper were each doing their best to *wake the captain* of their organizational ship. In the case of Watkins and Cooper, they risked their reputations and careers for fellow employees and shareholders. Rowley's actions were on behalf of every American citizen.

Thankfully, nonprofit leaders are unlikely to ever find themselves in so glaring a spotlight as Watkins, Rowley, and Cooper. But because of their public nature, nonprofits can be glass houses surrounded by rock throwers. Just ask the American Red Cross, after the public-relations fiasco over disbursement of the donations for the families and victims of 9/11.

So what lessons can we learn from these women?

- As John Gardner writes, "Never confuse status with leadership." Leadership is not a position or place of authority. As for personal accountability, the buck stops with each individual.

- Each individual must remain vigilant and when sensing the ship is veering off course, take the responsibility to take the appropriate action even though the con-sequences may be severe.

- We must always be motivated by what is best for our organization, not just for ourselves. We have an obligation to all crew members when encountering the rougher seas of our voyage.

When things go wrong in an organization, the first action is to look for someone to blame. Even in perilous times, however, the conscientious captain never blames his crew; nor does a loyal and competent crew member deny his responsibility to others. Even if the captain fails or refuses to accept responsibility, the members of the crew still do not have the luxury to "give up their own inner sense of captaincy" or to rationalize that the ultimate responsibility lays elsewhere.

Rowley, Watkins, and Cooper did not quit knocking when their captains refused to be awakened. When their captains would not respond, these loyal crew members did not just return to their cabins and say, "Well, I tried." Instead, they reached deep inside themselves and found their own *inner sense of captaincy*. In the end, the American public may never fully know how much we owe these three women for being so gutsy and incorruptible.

In recognition of their extraordinary courage, persistence, and resilience, *Time* magazine named the three women as "Persons of the Year," with their photographs displayed on the cover of the December 30, 2002/January 6, 2003 edition. One of the questions the Time interviewer asked was, "If the culture comes from the top, how is it that you three didn't fall prey to it?" In responding, Ms. Cooper said simply, "I think it comes back to the values and ethics that you learn through your life."

If on some darkened night you discover that your ship is sailing toward danger, will you make the effort to wake your captain? And if the captain still sleeps, will you be prepared to lead your crew to safety?

These are tough questions with no easy answers, but it is how we perform our everyday tasks, make our routine decisions, and the way we treat people on a daily basis that establishes who we are and what we are about. It is what we learn from these incidental and sometimes even trivial tests that increases our capacity to find our own *inner sense of captaincy* when the inevitable crisis comes.

CREDIBILITY

"Leadership Lite is the figment of a dull imagination."
                                        –Robert A. Floyd

"A reputation for a thousand years may depend upon the conduct of a single moment."
                                        –Ernest Bramah

On July 2, 1863, on a rocky hilltop outside the small crossroads town of Gettysburg, Pennsylvania, Federal troops held the high ground.

The commander of those Union troops on Little Round Top was not a typical army officer; he was a university professor. Colonel Joshua Lawrence Chamberlain commanded the 20th Maine and had been ordered by his superior to hold his position at all costs.

The 20th repelled charge after charge by a valiant 15th Alabama. Desperately running out of ammunition, the Maine men scrounged among their dead comrades but were down to a last few rounds.

It was highly unlikely they could resist one more Rebel attack; one third of the 20th Maine had fallen in the first hour and a half. And then in a moment of great courage and leadership, Chamberlain gave the command made famous in Michael Sharra's Pulitzer-Prize-winning book, *The Killer Angels*, and the movie *Gettysburg*: "Bayonets!"

As the weary Rebels charged again, Chamberlain raised his saber and led his men down the hill with fixed bayonets. Caught by surprise, the tired, valiant Confederates broke, wavered, and ran for their lives. The remaining Union soldiers had held Little Round Top.

Joshua Lawrence Chamberlain received the Congressional Medal of Honor for his bravery at Gettysburg. He survived the War to serve four terms as governor of Maine.

What persuaded the men of the 20th Maine, out of ammunition, to follow their leader down that hill to an uncertain fate? Did they suddenly make up their minds that this was a leader they could trust, in what must have seemed to them to be a suicidal mission?

During the previous year, the 20th Maine had fought with Chamberlain at the disastrous Union defeat at Fredericksburg, where he had lain throughout the freezing night under the body of a dead Union soldier. On the march leading to Gettysburg, the Colonel walked alongside his men leading his horse.

This quiet, soft-spoken scholar had been walking his talk from the day he was commissioned an officer in the Army of the Potomac. He had established his credibility and earned the trust of his men. When the critical time came to order "Bayonets!" his men dutifully fixed their bayonets and followed their leader down Little Round Top to victory.

A leader's credibility is largely measured by the consistency between his words and deeds. The old maxim "Actions speak louder than words" may be true, but from the standpoint of a leader, the actions and the words must be closely aligned. It is DWYSYWD (dwizzy-wid)—doing what you say you will do—that builds credibility between leaders and followers.

Leaders must have followers. Consistency, reliability, and trustworthiness are proven over time. In times of stability, these factors may not be as critical. But when crisis does come, if the leader has not established a trusting relationship with his people, it is unlikely he will have the credibility to mobilize his followers and devise a solid strategy to recover.

It is in the face of adversity that leadership credibility is tested. If prior to Little Round Top, Chamberlain's words had not been consistent with his actions, would his men still have fixed bayonets and followed him down that hill of death and uncertainty?

Credible leaders believe in the inherent self-worth of every individual. They demonstrate this by affirming others and by showing confidence in their followers. They may do this through delegating new responsibilities as well as by serving others. While they are interested in their own success, they are more interested in the success of the organization and their people.

Credibility is developed over time. It is like constructing a building—one brick at a time. Quality construction demands that there are no shortcuts.

✦✦✦✦✦✦

As hard as credibility is to build, it can be broken by only one inappropriate remark or action.

A lobbyist, for example, is hired to represent an organization or interest group before a legislature. I learned quickly that to be effective, a lobbyist must know their subject and be a skilled communicator. They should also be an expert in the legislative process and know how the bill they are promoting will affect each lawmaker and the lawmaker's constituents.

But communication skills, and knowing all the legislative nuances, are worth absolutely zero without a reputation for being straightforward and telling the truth.

Each day, while serving as a lobbyist for the Texas Motor Transportation Association, I entered the Capitol carrying my briefcase full of issue papers and all the necessary documents to support my group's position. I also

carried with me a much more precious cargo: my credibility.
I protected this cargo above everything else, because without
it, I had nothing.

There are no secrets under the Capitol Dome; one slip
of the tongue, one misstatement or lie, and the high-speed
Internet is no competition for word of mouth. I knew that my
career, my professional effectiveness, all boiled down to one
word: credibility.

✦✦✦✦✦✦

Trust and credibility are really two sides of the same
coin. The board of directors is the most powerful link
between the organization and its donors, constituents,
members, and stakeholders. It has the responsibility to
oversee that the words and deeds of both paid staff and
volunteer leaders are in constant alignment.

One way to build your own credibility is to not only take
your own values and ideas seriously, but also those of your
colleagues and peers. This is a critical attitude to take in any
organizational setting, but is especially important when you
are serving on a board of directors. You are not going to be
able to achieve your own goals and objectives without the
collaboration of others. Another strong reason to take your
colleagues and peers seriously is based on scientific findings;
research studies have shown that people tend to act consistently with our expectations.

"The implication for leaders," write James M. Kouzes
and Barry Z. Posner in *Encouraging the Heart: A Leader's
Guide to Rewarding and Recognizing Others*, "is that a
unified voice on values results from discovery and dialogue.
Leaders must engage individuals in a discussion about what
the values mean and how their personal beliefs and behaviors are influenced by what the organization stands for."

As a board member, you must engage your colleagues
in a dialogue that establishes common goals and values. At

times, you are sure to have different ideas and objectives, but honest dialogue often transcends personality differences and might possibly lead to common ground.

Maybe it will require a little old-fashioned horse trading, but creative leaders learn how to "walk in another's moccasins" by showing genuine respect and interest.

A leader must be willing to change perspective when circumstances change or when new information is introduced; not values, but perspective.

Have you ever noticed how your perspective changes when you are driving a car? If you find yourself behind a driver going 30 mph in a 40-mph zone, you see an idiot in the car ahead. If you are driving slowly, looking for an unfamiliar turn, the tailgater behind you is the idiot. Funny how the other guy is always the idiot.

An effective leader who changes his perspective when he gains new insight or information is not being wishy-washy; rather, he is exercising leadership by showing a willingness to learn from others. He knows he does not have all the answers and is not compromising his principles and values. An effective leader is always reaching out to discover better mousetraps; he would no more close his mind than he would close his door to stakeholders, constituents, and colleagues.

In the end, a leader is only as good as his word. If his words and deeds are consistent, he will form a bond with those he serves, a bond that will hold like Superglue as long as he does what he says he will do.

But that bond is also as fragile as precious crystal and must be handled with the utmost care.

DECISION-MAKING AND JUDGMENT

"There are few things wholly evil or wholly good. Almost everything ... is an inseparable compound of the two, so that our best judgment of the preponderance between them is continually demanded."
                                                    –Abraham Lincoln

"All my life whenever it comes time to make a decision, I make it and forget about it, and go to work on something else ... You've always got to keep going because there's always a decision just ahead of you that you've got to make ... If you make a mistake ... correct it by another decision, and go ahead."
                                                    –Harry S. Truman

On April 12, 1945, President Franklin D. Roosevelt died. at Warm Springs, Georgia. Vice President Harry S. Truman, the man who the New York Times later said was "... without

experience, without knowledge, without prestige," found
himself in a job he had neither sought nor desired.

In 1952, as he spent his last days in the White House,
he listened as Winston Churchill recalled their first meeting
in 1945. "I must confess, sir, I held you in very low regard. I
loathed your taking the place of Franklin Roosevelt. I
misjudged you badly. Since that time, you more than any
other man have saved Western civilization."

Not a bad compliment from one of the greatest leaders
of the 20th Century. One of Truman's leadership qualities
was the ability to decide—to make tough decisions in the face
of adversity. If he had not made the courageous decision to
drop the atomic bomb on Japan to end the war, I might have
been deprived of the love of my life. My future father-in-law,
who had just returned from Europe, was on leave waiting to
report to the West Coast where he and hundreds of thousands of other G.I.s would have been shipped to the Pacific
Theater for the invasion of Japan.

Truman also made the decision to begin the airlift to
overcome the Soviet Union's blockade of West Berlin. His
decision to send the Marshall Plan to a skeptical Congress
resulted in the economic recovery of Europe. He also moved
with swiftness to resist the Communist invasion of South
Korea. But as John Gardner writes, "Of course what was
involved was not only decisiveness, but also good judgment.
If all his moves had turned out badly, we would not be
praising his decisiveness."

✦✦✦✦✦✦

Gardner is right. Sound judgment is essential to effective decision-making. Effective decision-making is also
directly related to the characteristic of successful leaders who
willingly and objectively listen to others. President Truman is
famous for the nameplate on his desk, "The Buck Stops
Here," but he was equally on terms with "The Buck *Starts*

Here," meaning that he aggressively sought input from experts on the issue.

The leadership maxim, "We gain experience by making mistakes and we gain more experience by making more mistakes" is probably true, but hopefully in the process we learn not to repeat the same mistakes.

We also, with any luck, increase our decision-making and judgment capacities. "A key leadership skill is the ability to strip away the clutter and the noise and to focus on those few things that would have the greatest impact." As individuals we use our judgment and decision-making skills every day for such routine actions as the decision to get out of bed in the morning. With boards, the quality of decision-making directly correlates with the value being provided to stakeholders and constituents.

✦✦✦✦✦✦

Sound judgment and decision-making are magnified by the collective decisions made by boards of directors. Unfortunately, boards composed of individuals who have these key qualities don't necessarily have the same standard of quality in their collective decision-making. As reported in the *Harvard Business Review*, "Too often, the board of a nonprofit organization is little more than a collection of high-powered people engaged in low-level activities."

My experience in the profession bears this out. Boards must be willing to evaluate their competence as a board and be honest enough to admit when improvement is needed. If the board is displaying any of the following indicators, it is time to courageously evaluate board performance:

- Is the board experiencing difficulty in doing its work efficiently?
- Is the board having difficulty resolving issues or developing policy?

- Is the board unable to complete its agenda at a board meeting?

- Are there issues critical to the stakeholders for which no definitive position has been established or action taken?

- Are committee objectives unclear and/or often unrelated to the association's strategic plan?

- Are committee reports to the board often incomplete and not contributing information that board members need to take action on issues?

- Does the board have difficulty reaching consensus on key issues?

- Do some of the same issues keep coming up meeting after meeting, year after year, without the board being able to come to closure?

- Does the membership believe (perceptions are equal to reality) that the organization is not meeting its needs?

- Is the board getting the information it needs to make decisions about mission, strategy, programs, services, and finances?

- Is the board committed to improving its effectiveness?

The bottom line: One clear measurement of the effectiveness of a board of directors is its ability to make effective decisions—to be decisive on those matters and policies that hold the most meaning for their constituents and stakeholders. This is not about where to have the next meeting or what type of data-processing system should be bought. These are the type of administrative decisions that should be delegated to the staff.

Tough decisions involve considerable risk. As James M. Strock writes, "... they directly, understandably, and unavoidably implicate the vision of the organization. Whatever action is taken, or not taken, will have consequences for the core mission of the group." This might be an opportunity missed or a crisis ignored; it may be a decision that has immediate impact or far-reaching implications. But whatever the case, the decision is of sufficient magnitude that it requires dialogue, deliberation, and, in the end, decisiveness.

The good news is that decisive action taken at the right time can strengthen the board's ability to guide the fortunes of the organization. Decisive action, in fact, can be transforming, taking the organization to the next level of value for its beneficiaries. There is, of course, the possibility that the action may not be successful, but this risk can be mitigated by a methodical approach. "By aligning work and deeds," writes Strock, "decisive actions add predictability and certainty to an enterprise."

DIVERSITY: HONORING & APPRECIATING

"Individuals are different; in culture, color, ideas, and assumptions about the future. Individuals are alike; in their desire and right to be treated with respect and dignity."

–Robert A. Floyd

"The best leaders," writes Robert Rosen, "have a deep appreciation for people's differences." These differences are more than cultural, ethnic, and gender-based; they are also generational, religious, political, lifestyle, and personality based.

A leader must not only have an appreciation for diversity but a keen awareness of how differences can affect relationships, cooperation, and accomplishment of the mission. The advice given by Stephen Covey to "seek first to understand and then to be understood" is critical when serving on a board of directors with colleagues from different backgrounds.

In a 1999 environmental scan conducted by the American Society of Association Executives, one of the major findings was how generational and work-force issues were affecting trade associations and nonprofit organizations. The study found that among three different generations—Matures born before 1946, Baby Boomers, 1946-64, and Generation Xers, 1965-85—there were profound differences in attitudes and behavior that bear strongly on whether organizations can be successful. "There will be shifts in member perception of, and loyalty to, the association, differing preferences for programs and services, and differing degrees of volunteer involvement."

✦✦✦✦✦✦

When individuals with different experiences and dissimilar attitudes toward loyalty and volunteerism are combined with different communication and problem-solving styles, conflict is as likely as thunder following lightning. If these individuals are in key leadership positions, the possibility for a divided and dysfunctional board of directors is very real.

This first came to my attention during a strategic planning retreat I was facilitating for the board of a trade association. The association represented an industry whose members were prosperous business owners with at least two, and in some instances as many as three, generations working in the company. The industry was one of those where it was traditional to hand the business down from one generation to another.

While discussing governance during the SWOT analysis (strengths, weaknesses, opportunities, and threats), I asked if the governance structure was a strength or a weakness. The discussion was focused on the nomination, selection, and role of the organization's executive committee. It was apparent that the real decision-making took place within the nine-member executive committee.

The response to my question was quite mixed. Several stated the structure was a strength, but an approximately equal number argued it was a weakness. Those supporting the latter position were by far the most vocal.

Interestingly, those who saw the current structure as a strength were the older members of the board; those that saw it as a weakness were from the younger generation. I then began to carefully monitor the remainder of the SWOT analysis, and I discovered that the disagreements on almost all issues were due to generational differences.

In many cases the fathers (the older generation, all male) had stepped aside from the business operations, but to keep up their contacts and relationships with their industry friends, they remained active in the association. In particular, they formed a clique that controlled the organization's executive committee.

Several sons and daughters were serving on the board, but were frustrated that the board was essentially just a rubber stamp for the executive committee. To make matters even more divisive, the elders were strongly committed to the status quo, while their offspring wanted to offer new programs and services that would have a greater appeal to their own generation.

When I pointed this out to the participants, guess who agreed with my analysis and who did not? As far as I know, the situation is still the same and the generations remain at a standoff.

✦✦✦✦✦✦

I first became an enthusiastic supporter of equal rights for women on March 1, 1973, and doubled my enthusiasm on July 1, 1980. These dates just happen to correspond to the births of our two daughters, Kimberly and Leslie. I sought to act on this enthusiasm throughout my career by hiring women in key management positions. Three of my four deputy CEOs were women.

When I first joined TSAE, women were underrepresented on the board of directors and in leadership positions. The association, founded in 1928, had only elected one woman as board chair. With a sympathetic board and supportive nominating committees, we made great strides in increasing the gender diversity on the board. A second woman became board chair and women now compose almost fifty percent of the board's makeup.

I wish I could report that we made the same great strides in ethnic diversity, but this is not the case. We didn't, largely because the ethnic makeup of the organization (as well as the profession) is overwhelmingly white.

A diverse board does not assure effectiveness. And, yes, a diverse board can lead to divisiveness. On the other hand, a diverse board means that a wide range of ideas, perspectives, and experiences will enrich the deliberative process and lead to a much higher quality of decision-making.

An astute board member recognizes that each person may have ideas and skills that clearly distinguish him from his peers. The secret is to both appreciate these differences and to be aware of how these differences can be blended together to meet the goals and objectives of the organization.

A wise leader knows diversity can be a source of great strength and he is constantly looking for opportunities to bring out the best in everyone. Leaders who embrace diversity are better prepared to respond successfully to the myriad circumstances, situations, and changing conditions among their members and constituents.

EMPOWERMENT & ENCOURAGEMENT

"Tell me and I'll forget; show me and I may remember; involve me and I'll understand."
                                        –Chinese proverb

"An effective leader asks tough questions, of herself, of others. A wise leader knows there can be more than one right answer."
                                        –Robert A. Floyd

"Few things help an individual more than to place responsibility upon him, and to let him know you trust him."
                                        –Booker T. Washington

In *Leading People: Transforming Business from the Inside Out,* author Robert Rosen argues that people "want leaders with deeply-held human values who respect people's unique talents and contributions. They want leaders who will create an environment that nurtures excellence, risk-taking, and creativity."

According to Rosen:

- The best leaders have a deep understanding of power and participation ... they know that power increases when it is shared.

- Leaders must be willing to surrender authority, share ownership, and trust people's judgment.

- When people feel they are partners, they accept responsibility and take initiative.

- When people feel no emotional connection, they put in their hours and then go home.

At the center of an empowered organization is the principle that each individual has value; the seeds of empowerment are sown by a culture that respects the dignity of each individual. From respect grows trust, demonstrated by the leader whose words and deeds say: "I believe in you."

To illustrate, several years ago a large hospital allowed its nurses to make changes in the design of several patient-care units, changes the nurse thought would be both nurse-friendly and patient-friendly. The only requirement was that any changes met three criteria: they were cost-neutral, assured accountability, and improved the continuity of patient care.

First and foremost, people want to get the job done and done right; they want to be given the responsibility, held accountable, and allowed the freedom and flexibility to accomplish the task or project without having someone looking over their shoulders. In an empowered organization, workers know that when mistakes are made, they simply become teaching moments and not trials by fire.

"And most people," writes Skip LeFauve, "commit themselves to an effort only if they participate in the decision-making. Specifically, they must be involved in defining the problem and suggesting alternative solutions before they are asked to take action. In short, leaders must include people in decisions that affect them."

One of the most common and, I believe, destructive behaviors of well-meaning volunteer boards of directors, is micromanaging the professional staff. It is a surefire morale killer and can severely damage the relationship between the volunteer leaders and the staff to the point that the mission of the organization may suffer irreparable damage.

This is not about providing organizational and fiduciary oversight or establishing policies, which are both fundamental responsibilities of a board of directors. Rather, this is when any board member, or the board collectively, interferes in the day-to-day operations of the organization. Instead of empowering and building trust, the board becomes a source of frustration and tension.

Several years ago in Austin, Texas, a professional association had the reputation for being board-micromanaged.

Board members, committee chairman, and other volunteers just couldn't keep their hands off the day-to-day operations. This was a well-known fact in the community. In some instances, consultants actually reported to a committee and not to the executive director. The situation was so bad that the executive director turnover rate rivaled King Henry the Eighth's penchant for wives. Thankfully, the executive directors either just quit or were fired; none were beheaded!

After finally admitting that, year-by-year, more stuff was hitting the fan, a group of the association's leaders formed a task force to address the issues of staff turnover and board interference. Along with several association leaders, I was interviewed by the task force. Itold them I didn't know any professional executive in Austin who would go to work for them, short of an ironclad contract and a high six-figure salary.

To their credit, the task force recommended major changes later approved by the board. The organization has been stable for several years, *and* without a change in the chief executive officer. Things may not be perfect, but certainly the environment has substantially improved. The organization is no longer seen as an example of management *de jour.*

Even the most well-meaning boards and members must guard against this natural tendency to want to be hands-on. Hire the right leader, hold them accountable, but empower them with the capacity to lead the organization in the direction that has been established through well-crafted goals and policies.

✦✦✦✦✦✦

Now let's bring in the other "E," encouragement. It's vital for every leader to be aware that encouragement has the power to change lives. "We can't think of a better way to start the day," write James Kouzes and Barry Posner, "than to offer some encouragement. Why not set a positive tone bright and early by expressing how much you appreciate the contributions of others?"

Why not? What is there to lose? Perhaps only your best and brightest. Encouraging, empowering, and enabling are in, and command, control, and intimidation are out, even in the military or government bureaucracy. General Colin Powell's philosophy was "I am going to fight for you. I am going to do everything I can to make your job easier." That was certainly not the U.S. Army that I remember.

As Powell says, "The effective leader believes his or her people are competent ... the effective leader puts people in positions where they can excel and grow—and of course tracks, tracks, and encourages their progress ... "

✦✦✦✦✦✦

From my first day of work for TMTA on June 18, 1973, to our most recent conversation, my mentor and first real

boss, Terry Townsend, CAE, has encouraged me and
enabled me to be more than I ever thought possible. In the
thirteen years under his guidance, he never once told me *no*
when I asked for more responsibility or a new assignment.

When I messed up, he helped me clean it up and learn
the lesson. He was a firm, but gentle, teacher.

Believing in others may well be the strongest kind of
encouragement you can give. By saying, "I believe in you," a
leader sends a powerful message to his followers.
Communicating positive expectations is a powerful moti-
vator, whether in the family, the classroom, the work place,
or serving as a volunteer.

People want to succeed—and they need to succeed.
Volunteer leaders are no different, even though they do not
expect to earn more or be paid more in the traditional sense.

Volunteers, however, do seek fulfillment by
contributing to a cause greater than themselves. Their payoff
comes in knowing they have made a difference. While they
are not seeking recognition for its own sake, they still have
the desire to be acknowledged, appreciated, and given credit
for their good works.

The Salvation Army has 3.3 million dedicated volunteers who are "converted" to service. A key reason why the
Army has been so successful in recruiting and keeping
volunteers is the clear message they receive throughout their
service: volunteers are not just an adjunct to the organization; they are essential to the mission. Knowing that your
organization considers you *essential* to success not only
encourages you to go the extra mile, but you are very likely
to encourage others to take the trip with you.

In their book, *Encouraging the Heart: A Leader's
Guide to Rewarding and Recognizing Others*, Kouzes and
Posner list "The Seven Essentials of Encouraging":

1. Set clear standards.
2. Expect the best.

3. Pay attention.

4. Personalize recognition.

5. Tell the story.

6. Celebrate together.

7. Set the example.

As the saying goes, they don't care how much you know until they know how much you care. They are every person you interact with, on and off the board.

I would add to the list above: Give them freedom to make mistakes. If your people know that a mistake made while learning and growing will not be punished, they will feel more empowered to take risks, to test new ideas, to find more creative solutions.

One of the toughest challenges a leader faces is deciding when to turn over a project or responsibility to a subordinate, who may not be quite ready. But how else do they become ready? A leader who acts in this manner is saying, "I trust you; I think you can do it." And if the person has seen you empower others, watched you tolerate others' mistakes, and offer help when needed, then you have most likely created a new path for a leader-in-the-making.

Empower your people, encourage them, and then be pleasantly surprised when performance and results show measured improvement.

ETHICS

"Ethics, too, are nothing but reverence for life. ... good consists in maintaining, promoting, and enhancing life ... destroying, injuring, and limiting life are evil."
                                                    –Albert Schweitzer

"We have committed the Golden Rule to memory; let us now commit it to life."
                                                    –Edwin Markham

Ethics has become a buzzword in the organizational lexicon; perhaps because it seems so obvious, but unfortunately also because of the corporate scandals of the last two years. If there is any good news in the corporate scandals, it is that they validate ethics as integral to business decision-making. "An essential quality of professionalism," writes Bowen McCoy, "is an enduring ethic that causes the public in general to trust a person's work. ... Such leadership was lacking not only in Enron, but in its *board of directors* and the professionals who advised the firm." McCoy argues that the reason the American people became so indignant so quickly about the revelations, is that they saw the breaking of public trust.

Plug the keyword "ethics" into Amazon.com and you will get 5,116 hits. Universities have introduced undergraduate and graduate programs in ethics. Professional journals are ripe with articles on professional, business, and political

ethics. From the perspective of board service, I like what
Peter Koestenbaum says about ethics:

- Ethics means teamwork, understanding that effective leadership involves accomplishing tasks
  through people working together ... and remaining
  loyal to the group.
- Ethics is meaning. Meaning in your own work and
  in the work that you create for others.
- Ethics is love, compassion, service, and validation.
  It also means seeing the world from the other
  person's point of view.
- Ethics is tied to core values. The ethical person is
  motivated by what is right; not by what feels good.

While the corporate scandals were still front-page
news, I made a presentation on leadership to a nonprofit
organization whose members were the board chairs of agricultural cooperatives. As I flashed the photo of one of the
corporate crooks during my PowerPoint presentation, I
made the following observation:

If the agricultural cooperative had conducted a board-
approval survey of their members prior to the corporate
scandals, and then a follow-up while television continued to
beam the story into the members' living rooms, I would be
willing to bet a large steak that the board's approval rating
would have dropped. This was pure speculation on my part
and yes, I was using the issue to make a point. However, (1)
guilt is often by association, (2) public perception can be
more powerful than reality, and (3) fairness has nothing to
do with it.

My modus operandi was both extreme and speculative.
I was trying to impress upon these farmers and ranchers that
ethics is never negotiable and the mere perception of wrongdoing can undermine constituent trust, even if your organization is not remotely connected. As Benjamin Franklin said

so eloquently, "Let no pleasure tempt thee, no profit allure thee, no persuasion move thee, to do anything which thou knowest to be evil; so shalt thou always live jollily; for a good conscience is a continual Christmas."

"We believe our first responsibility is to ... all who use our products and services," reads the credo of Johnson & Johnson, the giant pharmaceutical company. In 1982, based on this credo, CEO James Burke, made an immediate decision that set a new standard for crises involving product tampering. After several people died from cyanide-laced Tylenol capsules, he ordered a recall of more than 31 million bottles, at a cost of more than $100 million.

With this decision, Johnson & Johnson lost millions of dollars. But by doing so, they demonstrated an ethical concern for their customers and the public over their financial bottom line. Too bad this message was missed by the failed executives of Enron, WorldCom, Global Crossing, et al; the only connection they ever made with Ben Franklin was a pocketful of hundred-dollar bills.

FLEXIBILITY

> *"When I saw this short, fat guy stretch a band*
> *between his toes ... Got that rubberband, uh! Upon*
> *his toe. And then he wriggle it up, all around his*
> *nose. You never heard a sound like the rubberband,*
> *Rubberband man, rubberband man ... "*
> –"Rubberband Man," The Spinners

Since I began my lobbying career almost 30 years ago, I have learned many lessons never taught in my college political-science classes. One particular lesson that has special implications for serving as a volunteer leader is the need to be flexible.

If you are attempting to influence a lawmaker's vote, you will soon learn that the ability to be flexible is the difference between keeping and losing your sanity in the twists and turns of the legislative process. Here's a story about a retired U.S. Marine colonel who was hired to lobby after spending 30 years in the service.

He was a good man and a decorated veteran, but flexibility was not one of the skills he learned in the Marines. Discipline, yes; flexibility, I don't think so. To give him credit, he tried, but he lasted only one legislative session and spent most of those 140 days being miserable.

He could never quite adjust to the fact that meetings don't always begin on time, that appointments are often changed or broken and, when it comes to taking orders, there is a difference between elected legislators and his

former subordinates. Let's just say he did not have a high
tolerance for ambiguity.

Not only are volunteer organizations loaded with ambiguity: there can be a diverse set of lifestyles, experiences,
ages, and attitudes. Mix these ingredients into a board of
directors, and a volunteer leader's ability to be flexible
becomes paramount.

Leaders must be willing to embrace uncertainty, not
shy away from it. One tip for dealing with uncertainty and
ambiguity is to avoid approaching new challenges with an
"either-or" mindset.

The *Center for Creative Leadership* encourages
leaders to be *both and* people by looking for creative answers
that can rightfully balance competing interests. You cannot,
of course, always have it both ways, but a leader who respects
all sides and disavows a rush to judgment is going to be a key
player when complex challenges confront the group.

A flexible leader is open to change, new ideas, and
new information, and able to adapt behavior, attitudes, and
work strategies in response to new information, changing
conditions, or unexpected obstacles.

A word of caution, however: don't be surprised if, by
showing flexibility on an issue, the true believers criticize
you for being wishy-washy or not sticking to your principles.

Those Luddites, who have not let a new idea penetrate
their stone wall since the first grade, will shriek like
banshees; it never ceases to amaze me that some groups and
individuals think *compromise* is a dirty word. Our Founding
Fathers built compromise into the U.S. political system from
the beginning; a principle of democracy is the give-and-take
of ideas and issues. Flexibility is not a sign of being indecisive or weak; rather it is an acknowledgement of the diversity
of ideas and the recognition that there is often more than
one right answer.

An esteemed colleague of mine, Christopher Williston,
CAE, asked this question when he was TSAE Chair: "Can

consensus be reached without compromise? Not likely ...
volunteer leaders have a tendency to take ownership for positions that they believe are in the best interest of the organization without regard to ... soliciting input and feedback from
other stakeholders."

There is a mountain of difference between being flexible on tough issues and practicing "leadership by polls," as
many politicians do to achieve their number-one priority of
getting elected, and their number two priority, staying
elected. In seeking to resolve differences through listening
and learning, the flexible leader keeps an open mind while
searching for more than one right answer. The politician,
with his public opinion polls in hand, shifts his position to
find whatever answer has the most voter appeal.

If by now you remain unconvinced that flexibility is a
genuine leadership skill, you have never had teenagers
under your roof. After I forbid my daughter to go to school
wearing a dress which bore a strong resemblance to a
negligee, she told me, in outrage, that I was "stupid, hard-
headed, and raised in the fifties."

To which I answered, "No dear, you are quite wrong. I
was actually raised in the sixties; and to prove to you that I
can be flexible, you can wear your nightgown around the
house any time you choose."

FORESIGHT

"Business more than any other occupation is a continual dealing with the future; it is a continual calculation, an instinctive exercise in foresight."
                                        –Henry R. Luce

"The hardest thing in life to learn is which bridge to cross and which to burn."
                                        –David Russell

In 1864, during the Civil War battle of Spotsylvania, Union General John Sedgwick was observing the ongoing battle. He turned to an aide and remarked, "They couldn't hit an elephant from this dist ... " Unfortunately for the General, the Southern gunners were more accurate with their cannon than he was with his opinion. He would have definitely earned an "F" for foresight.

In one of the best studies of leadership qualities, Credibility: *How Leaders Gain and Lost It, Why People Demand It*, authors James Kouzes and Barry Posner found that "forward-looking" was one of the four top characteristics of admired leaders. In fact, forward-looking (vision) was second only to "honesty" among those polled.

Countless tomes exist on the subject of vision, but one definition that I particularly like is from the work of Rosamund Stone Zander and Benjamin Zander in *The Art of Possibility: Transforming Professional and Personal Life.*

"A vision," writes the Zanders, "is a framework to take operations of an organization of any size ... into the areas of possibility ... a vision articulates a possibility ... a long line of
possibility relating outward."

A forward-looking board member is an informed
board member. They are constantly conducting their own
environmental scan of economic, social, political, and demographic issues that may impact future organizational success.
For example, a trustee of a school district needs to be aware
of demographic and property-value trends that will impact
the number and location of schools. This may involve future
expansion or even downsizing.

Similarly, the volunteer leader of a trade association needs
to be aware of how changes in market competition and government regulation may affect the profitability of the members.

Boards must be especially on guard during periods of
uncertainty and economic turbulence for possible intramural
quarrels within the organization or community. The following
check-list of symptoms may indicate real problems ahead and
more often than not, these symptoms are often linked
together. According to Management Consultant Glen Tecker,
where one exists, it is likely that others are also at work.

- Absence of clear definition of success between
  members of the board and/or between members of
  the board and staff
- Personal bias of influential members
- Business environment of members in chaos
- Turf protection, creating divisiveness.
- Only superficial issues discussed
- Short-term expediency vs. long-term benefits
- A lack of solid partnership among the people or
  groups in power
- Chaos expected in foreseeable future

- Unpredictable future creating anxiety
- Members having no sense of their future
- Internal squabbling
- Continuous conflict and confrontation
- Energy internally directed and personality driven
- Lack of trust

Foresight includes having an awareness of the past history, present surroundings, and what may be waiting around the next turn of the organization's road. Peter Koestenbaum says a forward-looking leader functions in the way a helicopter does: "He or she flies high to get the big picture but can quickly zoom down into a specific trouble spot and attend to details." The leader constantly scans the horizon, but does not take their eye off the day-to-day operations.

An excellent illustration of both visionary and practical thinking can be found in a story about two unusual suspects, The Lone Ranger and Tonto:

The Lone Ranger and Tonto are camping in the desert, asleep under their tent. Some hours later, Tonto wakes his leader. "Kemo Sabe, look up and tell me what you see."

The Lone Ranger replies, "I see millions of stars."

"What does that tell you?" asks Tonto.

The Lone Ranger ponders for a minute. "Astronomically speaking, it tells me there are billions of galaxies and potentially many billions of planets. Astrologically, it tells me that Saturn is in Leo. Time-wise, it appears to be approximately a quarter past three.

"Theologically, it's evident the Lord is all-powerful and we are small and insignificant. Meteorologically, it seems we will have a beautiful day tomorrow.

"What does it tell you, Tonto?"

Tonto remains silent for a moment, then speaks. "Kemo Sabe ... someone has stolen our tent!"

✦✦✦✦✦✦

Each member of the board is responsible for contributing to a collective vision for the organization: a vision that is based upon research, constituent-involvement, planning, and deliberation; a vision that is the result of consensus building—not that everyone agrees on each and every detail, but there is a solid consensus; A vision that creates a framework that will take the operations of the organization from hope to possibility.

When consulting with boards on strategic planning, I encourage the members to set aside time to do a little "dreaming" *as a board*. This is an excellent idea I "borrowed" from an outstanding nonprofit planner, Doug Eadie. This exercise may require facilitation, but it should be noncritical, wide-ranging, and above all, *fun*. No decisions should be made, but rather share ideas frankly, and dream of possibilities that can lead to greater satisfaction, value, and meaning for the stakeholders.

Humility

"Oh Lord it's hard to be humble
When you're perfect in every way
I can't wait to look in the mirror
Cuz I get better lookin' each day."

–Mac Davis

"I believe the first test of a truly great man is
humility."

–John Ruskin

Your fellow members or neighbors elected you to serve on the board so you should definitely feel proud of your accomplishment. Leaders have a right to be proud of their organizations, their achievements, and to have time to enjoy the limelight. Regrettably, there are those that confuse an election with a coronation.

The old Mac Davis tune is a humorous parody of the first deadly sin: Pride, defined as the excessive belief in one's own abilities. The Book of Proverbs declares that "pride commeth before the fall." Although humility is seldom associated with leadership, it is a quality of highest character.

In a five-year study of major corporations, Jim Collins, author of *Good to Great: Why Some Companies Make the Leap and Others Don't*, discovered "one of the most damaging trends in recent history is the tendency (especially by boards of directors) to select dazzling, celebrity leaders ... ." The most effective leaders are those who "display a compelling modesty," while those "with gargantuan personal egos contribute to the demise or continued mediocrity of the company." The corporate scandals of 2001-02 bear strong witness to the key findings of Collins' research.

Former President Harry S. Truman viewed humility as a strength: "You can accomplish anything in life, provided that you do not mind who gets the credit." Anything is possible if you share the glory and spread the wealth of a job well done.

As a lobbyist, I can identify with a story told by former presidential speechwriter James Humes. In describing a particular senator, he said the man always had to buy two seats when he flew back to his home state—one for himself and another for his ego.

For those who mistakenly associate humility with weakness, Collins cites the example of President Abraham Lincoln as his role model for strength with humility. Lincoln never let his ego blind him from his primary ambition of preserving the Union and ensuring an enduring nation. Always the subject of criticism, Lincoln would often convert his critics by bringing them into his administration.

Those who mistook Mr. Lincoln's personal modesty, shy nature, and awkward manner as signs of weakness "found themselves terribly mistaken to the scale of 250,000 Confederate and 360,000 Union lives, including his own," says Collins.

On the opposing side in the Civil War, General Robert E. Lee was a leader who believed in taking risks and whose foremost battle strategy was to attack, attack, attack. Yet, when it came to people, he was a gentle individual who operated by suggestion rather than by direct orders whenever he could.

General Lee was a humble man; his character was not built on ego. He truly believed and demonstrated by his actions that to lead was to serve. As a leader he was challenged not to lift himself up to greatness, but to help others succeed.

Abraham Lincoln and Robert E. Lee were ferocious advocates for opposing causes during one of the darkest periods in our nation's history; but neither let their personal ambitions override the admiration they had for those under their commands. It would be difficult to find two historic leaders with greater courage, passion, and desire to win than Lincoln and Lee; yet each remained in complete control of his ego and each personified humility as a leadership strength.

✦✦✦✦✦✦

Early in my association career, I was privileged to meet a leader who exemplified professionalism, poise, and humility. I had flown to Houston one evening with three other association executives to do an abbreviated form of "Association Management 101" for a group of about 20 young association executives.

My subject was government relations, and I had all of two years experience as a lobbyist. Arriving at the Austin airport, I met up with my three colleagues, one of whom I had never met. He cordially introduced himself as Linc Williston with the Texas Medical Association. We didn't visit much on the 40-minute flight, but I couldn't help but notice how friendly Linc was and that he was a good listener.

Before beginning his presentation, Linc distributed a handout that included an outline of his presentation so his audience could carefully follow his remarks. He then proceeded to give the most professional presentation I had ever heard. He was organized, knew his subject thoroughly, and treated his audience with total respect. Even though he had years of experience, he spoke as if talking to peers. I was in awe of his poise, confidence, and knowledge. His 30 minutes flew by, and then it was my turn.

With hastily-scratched remarks on a legal pad, no handouts, and making my first appearance before a TSAE audience, I stumbled and mumbled through what was to be

68 COURAGE TO LEAD

one of the most *forgettable* presentations in the history of association management. The group was gracious enough not to doze off and I cut their misery short by finishing early.

Totally embarrassed, on the flight back to Austin I resolved to never be that unprepared again. I also told myself that if I could even be one-half the professional that Linc Williston was, then I had a chance to be successful in my career.

Over the years, my admiration for Linc continued to grow. He led with great dignity, compassion, and integrity. He received virtually every honor his own organization and the association profession could bestow. Yet he was always humble and respectful toward others.

Linc was President and Chief Executive Officer of the Texas Medical Association. TMA is the professional organization for physicians, individuals not known for their humility or lack of ego. Yet, Linc was their CEO for 37 years and he enlarged and dignified the lives of others.

For the last eleven years of his life, Linc waged a courageous battle against chronic lymphocytic leukemia and lymphoma. He never complained nor lost his smile. When death came on February 1, 1999, Linc Williston, CAE, left a legacy of decency, humility, and a love for his profession and his fellow man.

To be a valuable volunteer leader, you must let your abilities, not your ego, guide you toward your objectives. You can be secure in your own self-confidence and do not have to always be right to satisfy your own inner needs. Like President Truman, you share the credit, knowing this is not only good citizenship but also good strategy. Humility is a leadership strength, never a weakness.

HUMOR

> *"(A) sense of humor can be a great help ... A sense of humor is part of the art of leadership, of getting along with people, of getting things done."*
>
> –Dwight D. Eisenhower

> *"Any fool can make things bigger, more complex, and more violent. It takes a touch of genius–and a lot of courage–to move in the opposite direction."*
>
> –Albert Einstein

> *"In order to keep a true perspective of one's importance, everyone should have a dog that will worship him and a cat that will ignore him."*
>
> - Dereke Bruce

My friend Bob Lively is an ordained minister, teacher, writer, and master storyteller. He tells one of my favorite stories about the brash young man taking his beautiful blonde date on a drive in his shiny new convertible. After driving the pleasant country roads, he suddenly realizes they are lost. Seeing a farmer behind an old mule plowing his field, the young man stops his car, honks several times, and then yells, "Hey, old man, where is the road to Austin?"

The farmer never looks up from his plowing. Again, honking his horn, the young man yells, "Hey, old man. Are you deaf? Where is the road to Austin?" The farmer continues to ignore him.

His anger rising, the young man yells, "Hey old man, if you don't tell me where the road to Austin is, I'm going to jump over this fence and get in your face!" The farmer continues his work without looking up.

To impress his date, the young man jumps over the fence, runs up to the farmer and, inches away from his face, screams, "Old man, you better tell me where the road to Austin is or else!"

The farmer wipes his sweaty brow, reaches into his hip pocket, pulls out an old colt revolver, and puts the end of the barrel in the young man's face.

From his somewhat subjective perspective, the barrel looks more like a cannon to the young man, who begins to sweat profusely. The farmer smiles and says, "Young man, I am going to show you the road to Austin, but first I have one question. Have you ever kissed a mule's behind?"

"Noooo," the young man stuttered. "But I've always wanted to!"

If conflict erupts and you can ease the tension with a light moment and without embarrassing anyone, you have the key to renewing the spirit of cooperation. Humor, correctly used, is an effective springboard for calming frayed nerves.

The old adage that we should take our issues or causes seriously, but not ourselves, is correct to a point. We should not, however, take our cause so seriously that it blocks out our fair-mindedness, objectivity, and civility. Perhaps a helpful reminder in tense situations is to look into our own mirror and see which end of the mule is reflecting back.

President Ronald Reagan had a great sense of humor and was especially good at turning the humor on himself. While waiting for surgery after being shot outside of the Washington Hilton Hotel in 1981 he said to his wife Nancy, "Honey, I forgot to duck." He also quipped, "I hope all of these doctors are Republicans."

Immediately following the shooting, Reagan's popularity soared to 85%. A year or so later, however, after the economy had gone sour, it had fallen to 32%, which his pollster, Richard Wirtham, lamented was about as low as it could go. Reagan, ever the optimist, said, "Oh, Dick, for God's sake, stop worrying or I'll just go out and try to get shot again."

I served on the school board in the mid-eighties, a period of rapid growth, with spiraling building and land costs. One tough decision led to another and to the potential for conflict and disagreement among the seven members. But differences of opinion never led to raised voices or finger-pointing because each member, as well as the superintendent, was blessed with a splendid sense of humor.

When I ran for a second term, I was unopposed, as was my good friend and fellow board member, Joe Kocks, who was seeking his fourth term. When the votes were totaled, I had out-polled Joe by one vote. At the next board meeting, I announced that I just couldn't bring myself to vote for Joe; it brought the house down. Joe laughed harder than anyone.

Having a sense of humor doesn't necessarily mean that you tell great jokes or are naturally witty; it means that you have the ability to laugh at yourself and find humor in events and people. A little self-deprecation can go a long way to puncturing a tension-filled balloon that is rising from lack of clarity or a misunderstanding.

The right touch of humor at the proper time can be a valuable leadership tool, when used with care. You should never use it to ridicule or to belittle a colleague or his position on an issue. A sense of humor is a great gift and boards are in need of leaders who know how to melt the ice with a few rays of humorous sunshine.

INSPIRATION

"His triumphs exceed his success."
-Poet Laureate Robert Pinsky
on Sandy Koufax

*"Success is not measured by what you accomplish
but by the opposition you have encountered, and
the courage with which you have maintained the
struggle against overwhelming odds."*
-Orison Swett Marden

Closing his shoeshine stand for the evening at the Grand
Hyatt Washington, the man saw me and very pleasantly told
me to sit down. I protested mildly, but I really did want my
boots shined before dinner. Before he got his polish back
out, he had already earned a generous tip.

To initiate conversation, I asked his opinion of the big
Washington-Dallas game. With a very pronounced accent,
the shoeshine man said he really didn't care for American
football—his sport was soccer and he also enjoyed karate.
Born in France, he had left his home on Africa's Ivory Coast
17 years earlier to come to the United States.

He then mentioned that his son played basketball and
began a story that kept me mesmerized until my boots were
ready for an evening out.

His son, on a full scholarship at a nearby university, had
been recruited by several schools and talked about playing in
the pros. But Dad had other plans. Only a few players make

the pros. Dad's advice was to enjoy his four years and then go to medical school. The man said this with such conviction that I had little doubt the son was a future doctor.

Admittedly, it is not so unusual for a man in his position to have a son that excels in sports. And from the man's build, it was possible that he also had been an accomplished athlete.

The son was not his only child. An older daughter had just received her undergraduate degree and was now in pharmacy school. He had surprised her at her college graduation with a brand new car—keeping his promise made four years before.

By now I was hooked. This man was an extraordinary individual. I asked him how long he had been working at the Grand Hyatt, where I frequently stayed while visiting Washington. Eleven years, he replied, but he had actually had a shoeshine business managing multiple employees. Now, however, he was shining shoes himself to give him more time to go back to school!

By now I realized nothing should surprise me, but I had to ask what he was studying. Again, he responded very gently that he had a master's degree and was pursuing a PhD in macroeconomics! With his thick accent, it might have been "micro," but it was out of my league either way.

During my time on his stand, I observed a steady stream of Hyatt employees pass by, some in uniform, others in coat and tie. Not one employee passed by without calling his name, and he turned to give each one an equally friendly greeting. It was apparent this was a man people both liked and respected.

My mind wandered to the previous day and to a technology seminar I had attended. As we waited for one of the breakout sessions to begin, my tablemates and I traded business cards. One colleague, noticing my tagline "Leadership and Management Consulting," asked if I taught leadership. I said that I did my best to point people in the right direction.

I do believe leadership principles can be taught, and I believe leadership can be learned. And while some people inherit stronger genes than others, I have my doubts about *natural born leaders.*

Position and authority are no guarantees of leadership. We all know people in high places who will never earn the respect of their people.

On the other hand, there are many skilled and dedicated individuals who may not be the CEO or even a department head, but who are definitely leaders. They exhibit competence, vision, trustworthiness, and credibility. These people have become leaders not by status but by performance.

As I watched the man buff my boots to a high shine, I knew I was in the presence of an authentic leader. I handed him the twenty-dollar bill with absolutely no intention of receiving change. For the past twenty minutes I had received a lesson in leadership that was worth much, much more.

I felt truly revitalized as I headed back to dress for the evening. Here was a most uncommon man doing a common task, but for him it was merely a means to a greater end.

Leadership is not a place, but it can be found in unexpected places. In the Grand Hyatt Washington, I found not only a leader who literally shines, but also an example of shining leadership.

INTEGRITY

*"If you have integrity, nothing else matters. If
you don't have integrity, nothing else matters."*
　　　　　　　　　　-Former U.S. Senator Alan Simpson

*"One of the most universal cravings of our time
is a hunger for compelling and creative leadership
... The crisis of leadership today is the mediocrity
or irresponsibility of so many of the men and
women in power, but leadership rarely rises to the
full need for it."*
　　　　　　　　　　-James MacGregor Burns

Although James MacGregor Burns could have written the
above words yesterday, he wrote them a quarter century ago
in the prologue to his Pulitzer-Prize-winning classic,
Leadership. In the past two years, even though we have had
glimpses of compelling leadership (President George Bush
and Mayor Rudy Giuliani), most of the nation's attention has
been focused on leadership mediocrity and irresponsibility.

- One of the most powerful religious figures in the
  nation refuses to acknowledge dishonorable
  conduct on his watch, literally crimes against children, and is finally forced out in humiliating
  disgrace. His good works are overshadowed by his
  stubborn refusal to be held accountable to his
  constituents.

- In the business community, a real-life Monopoly game was played by corporate thugs who collected millions by deceit and outright thievery. They hopefully will go straight to jail, collecting years of prison time and paying millions in fines. While breaking the law, they also broke the trust of their employees, shareholders, and communities.

- A United States Senator was forced from his lofty position of power after his lack of judgment and common sense became too much of a liability for even his own political party to bear.

- Even the nonprofit community has not been immune to poor leadership judgment and decision-making. The American Red Cross had to be called on the carpet by the U.S. Congress before acknowledging the mishandling of donor contributions to the families and victims of 9/11.

++++++

Following the resignation of President Nixon in 1974 in the wake of the Watergate Scandal, Vice President Gerald Ford began what was to be a very short tenure as President. Yet during his brief time in office, he restored honor and respect to the White House. "First and foremost," writes David Gergen, "he affirmed the importance of honesty among our elected leaders. 'Truth is the glue,' Ford said, and he proved it every day he was in office."

Integrity and honesty are closely aligned. Honesty is not limited to financial matters, but rather encompasses all that a person is and does. Honesty is being true to self and to others. Honesty is sharing credit for the victories and taking responsibility for the defeats. Honesty is to leadership as the Sun is to our existence.

During his lengthy career in public service, Gergen
served on the White House staff of four American Presidents:
Richard Nixon, Gerald Ford, Ronald Reagan, and Bill Clinton.
In his book on presidential leadership, *Eyewitness to Power:
The Essence of Leadership Nixon to Clinton,* Gergen writes
that "Richard Nixon and Bill Clinton were two of the most
gifted presidents of the last 30 years." Nixon was an excellent
strategist and made the daring move to open doors to China.
Clinton was an excellent political tactician.

"Yet," writes Gergen, "each was the author of his own
downfall. Nixon let his demons gain ascendance, and
Clinton could not manage the fault lines in his character.
They were living proof that before mastering the world, a
leader must achieve self mastery."

✦✦✦✦✦✦

It is difficult, if not impossible, to hide a person's true
character very long beneath the veneer of a warm and winning
personality. If, behind the mask of a pleasing personality, the
character is flawed, any trust that might have been established at
one time will ultimately be destroyed.

If character is integrity-based, people will put their
faith in leaders who demonstrate that they place their own
interests behind those of their followers. Integrity is being
true to your word and your commitments; it cannot be faked.

LEARNING

"Learning is defined as a change in behavior. You haven't learned a thing until you can take action and use it."

–Don Shula and Ken Blanchard

"Lead by learning; learn by leading."

–Robert A. Floyd

My dad was a young boy when the Wright Brothers flew for a few seconds at Kitty Hawk on December 17, 1903. On July 20, 1969, he watched with fascination as Neal Armstrong took "one small step for man, and one giant leap for mankind," becoming the first person to walk on the moon.

Dad was a school administrator, farmer, and teacher. He particularly loved teaching science because he had a curious mind and always wanted to learn more about what made things tick: which new kinds of grasses were the most drought-resistant and why certain students from similar backgrounds could be so dissimilar in the classroom. He was a lifetime learner without ever knowing the term.

My own love of learning comes both from my mother and my father. My mother was the school librarian and taught Texas history. I love to read and I love history. With the exception of my family, my golden retrievers, and a few close friends, my favorite companions are books. When I travel to a new location, the first thing I do is search for the local bookstore.

Former New York Mayor Rudy Giuliani offers this advice about learning: "Developing your own expertise is not simply something you ought to do because it's your duty (though it is), or even because it's fun to know how these things work (it's that, too). It is also the best way to weed out the biases and pretensions among those who want to influence you ... Having your own knowledge gives you a frame of reference, helping you decide whether or not to trust the advice someone is giving you."

One certainty in all our uncertainty is this: our changing world makes continuous learning the key to survival. As one trade-association executive told me, "My industry is changing so rapidly that by the time your book is in print, what I told you may well be out-of-date."

An effective leader—whether the President of the United States or volunteer activist—must constantly develop new skills, fresh perspectives, and be willing to abandon old ideas and attitudes. In the words of Alvin Toffler: "The illiterate of the future will not be the person who cannot read. It will be the person who does not know how to learn."

Leaders have a *bias for action*, and learning is an act of leadership. The farmer elected to his agriculture cooperative's board needs to not only know all about the local challenges facing his friends and neighbors, but must now become aware of global markets.

While a newly elected school trustee has learned a great deal about the expectations of parents and taxpayers during the campaign, his learning about the school system has just begun. If his last course in accounting was Accounting 101, he faces a steep learning curve on the district's operating budget before he can make informed decisions.

The newly chosen hospital board member must learn the hospital's operations and financial condition, but if he is to effectively exercise his oversight responsibilities, he must become a student of the entire healthcare system. How will federal cutbacks in Medicaid affect the hospital's bottom line? What are the implications of a nationwide shortage of qualified nurses? In a litigious society, can physicians afford to carry malpractice insurance?

✦✦✦✦✦✦

I was once in the office of a business and economics professor at a major university. Since I make it my civic duty to support our national GNP by spending both an excessive amount of time and money at Barnes and Noble, Borders, and local bookstores, my eyes automatically wandered to the bookshelves lining his office. I'm always looking for titles to add to my reading list.

As I carefully studied his extensive collection of scholarly works and economic texts, I found only two or three recent titles. What truly amazed me was that less than half a dozen of his entire collection seemed to have been written in the last ten years.

This is not to say his collection was out of date; many of the books on economics and business were classics. But with all the changes that have taken place in the last ten years—technology, globalization, changing markets and demographics—his library seemed woefully lacking.

To give him the benefit of the doubt, my quick survey of his office was certainly not enough to indict the man for his lack of interest in learning, but in our conversation, I found him to be truly uninterested in being a lifetime learner.

He may be a great teacher and admittedly my research was shallow. However, I saw in him what my school-principal dad said about comparing two teachers: One had 30 years of experience because she had been deeply committed to giving her best to her students and to her own personal growth. The other had one year of experience, repeated 30 times, because she had a job.

To be a responsible steward/trustee of your organization, you must make the same dedicated commitment as teacher number one.

You must commit to increasing your own knowledge while fostering a learning environment at all levels of the organization. You should support continuing education and skill-building opportunities for the professional staff, knowing that an organization's performance depends on the productivity and performance of its employees.

Encourage your fellow board members to actively engage in improving their own leadership skills, both individually and collectively. In essence, as a leader you are endorsing the basic rationale for learning organizations set forth by Peter Senge in the *Fifth Discipline*: "In situations of rapid change only those that are flexible, adaptive, and productive will excel. For this to happen ... organizations need to discover how to tap people's commitment and capacity to learn at all levels."

A leadership study of CEOs conducted by the Center for Creative Leadership found that more than 70 percent of respondents read leadership books. In addition, they attend seminars, work with colleagues, join professional associations, and have professional coaching.

As you l*ead by learning*, you are expanding your capacity for creativity, innovation, dealing with change, and expanding your critical thinking skills. You are preparing yourself and your organization for whatever challenges may lie ahead.

LISTENING

"Listening is not a skill, it is a discipline."
                                                    –Peter Drucker

"My wife says I never listen to her … "
"At least that's what I think she said."
                        –Message on the front and back of a t-shirt,
                                                    seen at the mall.

At a small group meeting, a discussion became a debate as one person took a decisively different position from the others. Each member of the majority took turns trying to use "logic" to convince their fellow participant why they were right and he was wrong. One even offered to send the prodigal a book, which would obviously show him the path.

While the argument was not mean-spirited, it reminded me of the many times when if I had only shut up and listened—truly listened—to the other person, things might have turned out differently. One of the first rules for effective leaders, writes Dr. Stephen Covey, is to "seek first to understand and then to be understood."

When you find yourself at loggerheads with a colleague, and you just can't make him understand why you are right and he is so obviously wrong, one of the best techniques you can use to learn more about his concerns or motives is to ask questions. Real questions, that is, ones designed to increase your understanding of the situation and/or this person.

You have very little to lose with this approach and much to gain. First, you may actually learn something new and helpful. Second, you are likely to build a higher level of trust with this individual, even though the two of you still may disagree. Third, believe it or not, he just might be right!

An effective illustration of what true listening can accomplish comes from the corporate world but has equal application to any organization: nonprofit, for-profit, or public.

In the early 1990s when I was the President of the Texas Motor Transportation Association, our largest member, Central Freight Lines, was subject to a unionization vote by the Teamsters Union. This story, I would add, is about communications and not about union versus nonunion interests.

In the election, the Teamsters came within a bobcat's whisker of winning the vote in a state that has a strong right-to-work law. Central's management was shocked and realized this was a staggering wake-up call. If the environment and corporate culture didn't change, Central would face a future as a Teamsters organized company.

The company reached out to a retired trucking-company executive named Tom Clowe. Tom had been one of the most successful trucking-company CEOs in the state, had built and sold his company for a handsome profit and retired. His organizational and communications skills, however, would not allow him to stay in retirement.

For the next several months, Tom traveled thousands of miles across the state of Texas to walk the docks of Central's many terminals—mostly in the early-morning or late-evening hours when the docks were most active shipping and receiving the freight.

Although Tom is one of the best public speakers I know, he did little talking—instead he listened. At first the employees were suspicious of his intentions—no Central management person had really listened to their concerns and complaints in years. But gradually, he began to win their confidence as they saw he was a leader who not only listened, but walked his talk.

The results: A year or so later when the second election was held, the company won the election overwhelmingly and the Teamsters went home empty-handed.

++++++

Tom had applied one of the most critical skills a leader can possess if they are to be successful over the long term: the ability to practice empathic listening. Stephen Covey, the author of the best-selling *Seven Habits of Effective People*, says there are at least five levels of listening—ignoring, pretend listening, selective listening, attentive listening, and empathic listening. "Empathic listening is the most developed," writes Dr. Covey. "It is done with the eyes, ears, and heart."

Covey's central message is that communicating effectively requires that you first understand what the other person is saying before you try to explain your own position. Until you become adept at this, you will often find yourself at cross-purposes with the person you are dealing with.

Listening is about caring; it is not waiting impatiently for the next person to stop talking so you can offer your opinion or point of view. Listening to another person is one of the greatest gifts a leader can give. True listening says "I respect you and I am concerned about you."

And frankly, it is good business or political strategy. The better you can truly listen to what your fellow board members or staff are saying, the better you will understand where they are coming from and adjust your strategy accordingly. This only becomes manipulative when you are solely interested in advancing your own agenda and don't really care about the concerns of others.

As Tom walked the docks of Central Freight Lines, he obviously had an agenda that included defeating the Teamsters, but he knew this would only be accomplished by truly listening to and addressing the concerns of the employees. He knew if Central was going to be profitable, its employees needed to be treated like true partners and not just some impersonal means to the company's ends.

Listening is up against some really tough competitors: busy-ness, distractions, unfiltered chatter and noise, and lives always on fast forward. You have to truly want to listen to the other person "with your eyes, ears, and heart," as Covey says. But the investment is worth it. "People who take the time to listen," write Richard J. Leider and David Shapiro in *Repacking Your Bags: Lighten Your Load for the Rest of Your Life,* "to each other's words and feelings make a priceless contribution to their relationship."

Brad Fregger, President of 1st World Library and the Author of *Get Things Done,* says the same thing a little differently, "Yes, you do know how to listen ... you do it often. You do it whenever you're with someone who is saying something that interests you ... you just choose not to listen at times."

He goes on to say that the true secret of effective listening is to encourage your inherent curiosity. It's when we are truly curious about the other person, what they think and believe, and why they think and believe the way they do, that we listen most effectively. "It's impossible to overstate the importance of curiosity. Only through curiosity do we gain understanding and, therefore, solve problems and resolve conflicts."

++++++

Former President Dwight D. Eisenhower is best remembered for being the Supreme Allied Commander in Europe during World War II and the commanding general who gave the orders to launch the Normandy invasion on June 6, 1944. What is less known about General Eisenhower is that he was selected to be head of the Allied Command over hundreds of others who were his senior in service. He did this by being a great listener.

Eisenhower knew how to listen and to ask the right questions. "As a military staff man for so many years," writes James C. Humes, "Eisenhower had learned to listen—and listen close and hard. Along the way he had a knack of seizing on others' words to serve his own ideas. He got his way by letting others take the credit."

In *The Road Less Traveled*, Scott Peck observed: "An essential part of true listening is ... the temporary giving up or setting aside of one's own prejudices, frames of reference ... so as to experience as far as possible the speaker's world from the inside ... The unification of speaker and listener is actually an extension and enlargement of ourselves, *and new knowledge is always gained from this.*" (My emphasis)

As a leader, you undoubtedly have your own ideas, goals and objectives; if you didn't, you would be at the mall or on the golf course. But you are dedicated to making the world a little better. Empathic listening, as much or more than your own verbal skills, will be the skill that helps you excel and establish the relationships that weather the worst storms.

MENTORING

"Never try to teach a pig to sing; it wastes your time and it annoys the pig."
                                                        –Paul Dickson

"A leader is always mentoring: leading by example, sharing knowledge, encouraging growth, accepting mistakes as part of the territory and refusing to take back the monkey."
                                                        –Robert A. Floyd

The best leaders are mentors. They mentor any place where there's an opportunity to help followers grow. Leaders are constantly aware of the mentoring moments when they can reach out to followers and help them develop their own leadership capacities. An authentic leader understands and accepts this as gospel and preaches it from dawn to dusk.

A leader's responsibility is to create other leaders. One of the greatest misunderstandings about leadership is that the only place it can be found is at the top of the organization. Nothing could be further from the truth—or more damaging to the long-term future of the organization than for leadership to remain isolated in the upper reaches of the organization.

A good friend, Jim Bearden, is a gifted public speaker. One of his top presentations is titled "Listen to Your Sergeants." As a young Marine officer, Jim was preparing to leave for his tour of duty in Vietnam. He asked his dad, a Marine Corps veteran, for his advice. "Listen to your sergeants" is the wisdom the father passed down to the son. He knew that in the military the sergeants are the one constant providing leadership from one combat engagement to another.

When do you learn best? When you are reading, listening to a keynote presentation, or participating in an educational seminar? None of the above. It is when you are facilitating the learning of others. When you are preparing a presentation, you are learning. When preparing lessons for my classes, I am at my learning best because I feel that I owe my students the best of my efforts.

Command-and-control organizations are not mentoring organizations. Those who believe in lifetime learning, and perhaps more importantly, in the lifetime learning of their employees and colleagues lead mentoring organizations. Commanding others and mentoring others are on opposite sides of the globe. One side is dark and discouraging; the other is light, inviting, and encourages the best and brightest minds to grow and blossom.

During my professional career, I was blessed with exceptional mentor-leaders. In my first association position, Terry Townsend, CAE, was a great mentor. He would only grab the rope when he saw that I was about to hang myself. It wasn't so much what he said; it was what he did. He mentored through role modeling and by allowing me to make mistakes, learn from them and grow. He was a great encourager.

One of my proudest accomplishments as a CEO is that over the years, four of my direct reports would each go on to lead a nonprofit organization and one would develop a successful business in the for-profit sector. In circumstances where they can't exert direct control, what good leaders do is teach others to be leaders.

A study conducted by the Center for Creative Leadership showed that corporate CEOs believe a central part of their job is to develop leaders in their organization. Almost all respondents (90.3 percent) indicated they are very or somewhat involved in leadership development in their organizations. They view leadership development as a key responsibility and an ongoing process. Employee development was ranked as the single most important challenge leaders will face in coming years.

If you have just been sworn in as a new board member, whether it was a mere formality or whether you had a tough, competitive election, it is unlikely that you are thinking of yourself as a mentor. Think otherwise.

I don't know what your gifts, talents, and skills are, but I do know that you have them or you would not have been chosen for your position on the board. You may have been elected by constituents who believed in your ability to improve the school system, nominated by peers with whom you've served on committees, or perhaps your passionate support of the cause brought you to the attention of members of the staff.

No matter. The fact you have been selected means that you bring something to the table that others consider to be of great value. Your responsibility, then, is to share your talents, knowledge, and expertise with others. You may not think of this as mentoring, but that is exactly what it is.

Your first mentoring assignment, therefore, is to be aware of the gifts you bring to the table and then to be vigilant for the mentoring moments when you can share your knowledge with others.

PASSION

*"Be not afraid of greatness: some are born great,
some achieve greatness and some have greatness
thrust upon them."*
                                    –William Shakespeare

*"Passion comes from what you contribute, rather
than what you get."*
                                    –Peter Senge

The writer Soren Kierkegaard writes: "If I were to wish for
anything, I should not wish for wealth and power, but for the
passionate sense of the potential, for the eye which, ever
young and ardent, sees the possible. Pleasure disappoints,
possibility never. And what wine is so sparkling, what so
fragrant, what so intoxicating, as possibility!" (My emphasis)

Passion is a key quality of leadership. Leading is a
tough job, so passion is a necessary ingredient to keep the
fires burning when setbacks outnumber victories, when
obstacles overshadow opportunities.

It's true. Feeling passionate about the cause is what
keeps us going when the pressures of time and tasks are
vying for our attention. I don't believe that an individual
awakens one morning, opens one eye at a time, and suddenly
decides to run for a trustee position on a school board out of
a long-festering desire for public service.

An individual, however, who feels passionately about
improving the educational quality in her community, makes

up her mind to sacrifice her time and donate her talents because she cares enough about giving her children and those of her neighbors the best education possible.

When association executive Leslie Midgley chose to chair the board of the local Alzheimer's organization, she did so because of her passionate commitment to help fight the disease that was agonizingly killing her mother.

Having passion does not mean that you must eat, sleep and, dream your cause 24/7, but it does means you have to really want to provide your services and share your talents for something you strongly believe in.

When he delivered his famous "I Have a Dream" speech from the steps of the Lincoln Memorial on August 23, 1963, Dr. Martin Luther King made a passionate appeal to all Americans to support the Civil Rights Movement.

With his arm extended around a retired NYC firefighter, President George Bush stood at Ground Zero and passionately expressed the feelings of an entire nation as he responded "We can hear you," to the crowd of heroes, loved ones, and survivors of the 9/11 attack on America.

Yet there are countless numbers of leaders at all levels across our country who may not receive the public recognition of Martin Luther King or President Bush, but who nonetheless bring their own strong passions to their work, avocations, and volunteer efforts. Passionate people believe so strongly in their cause or mission that they radiate an energy and enthusiasm that is contagious.

When I was selected to serve on the Board of Directors of the Texas Society of Association Executives, I brought a strong passion for serving an organization and profession that had been very good to my family and me. My passion to help volunteer leaders improve their leadership capacities to better serve their organizations and constituencies continues to run deep.

Why? Because I believe that volunteer board leaders, both nonprofit and public-sector, are positioned to do a great amount of good at all levels of society. Those who can add the most value to their communities and constituencies will be volunteer stewards who have developed and polished their leadership skills.

++++++

A little over five years ago, I received an email from a man I did not know, asking if he could have an hour of my time. Normally, I am pretty considerate, but due to whatever mini-crisis I was going through, I said I didn't have the time. He wrote back and thanked me for my candor.

Guilt soon got the best of me, so I called him back and offered to meet with him. That was a fortuitous meeting for me, and I've been blessed by my relationship with Barry Silverberg.

It would be hard to find two more different individuals; Barry is a transplanted Jewish New Yorker and I'm a Christian West Texan. But we soon discovered that we had much in common: our dry senses of humor, a tendency to be a touch irreverent, but most of all our passion for the nonprofit profession and the advancement of nonprofit boards.

In three short years, Barry has taken his dream of having a center to provide educational and supporting resources for nonprofits to the reality of the *Austin Community College Center for Nonprofit and Community Based Organizations*. To say he has been successful is like saying Joe Montana was a pretty fair quarterback.

Barry would be the first to say he hasn't done it alone, but his passion, vision, and commitment to excellence have collectively been the driving force behind the Center. Over the past three years the Center has conducted a full schedule of professional development seminars for nonprofit leaders and staff—and most at no charge. While ACC has underwritten the operating costs of the Center, Barry has recruited (badgered and cajoled) numerous experts in their fields to donate their time and talents *pro bono* to lead the vast array

of educational offerings. Saying *no* to Barry is like saying *sic'*
'em to a Rottweiler.

It's his commitment and enthusiasm that you can't say
no too. He radiates passion about the value of the social and
public-sectors through his work, teaching, and community
involvement. He serves on numerous nonprofit boards and
willingly and freely gives himself to the cause he believes in
so passionately. The only reason I would argue against his
cloning is his propensity for telling bad jokes.

✦✦✦✦✦✦

One slight caveat about passion: it is wonderful to have
passion about something you feel strongly about; however,
your passion should not prevent you from being open to the
thoughts and opinions of others. Passion should not blur
your objectivity and fair-mindedness.

Remember that you are just one leader in your organization. At the end of the day when your constituents measure
results, their evaluation will assess the collective effectiveness
of the board. Collaboration is the key; don't ever deny your
passion, but make sure it remains an asset and doesn't
become a liability.

PATIENCE

"Genius is eternal patience."
　　　　　　　　　　　　　–Michaelangelo

"The difference between greatness and mediocrity is often how an individual views a mistake."
　　　　　　　　　　　　　–Nelson Boswell

There are many folks, including my spouse, who would say that my writing about patience is like a vegetarian writing about the nutritional value of beef. I would argue with them, but then I don't have the patience. This is one area where I will always be in recovery, but the truth is I am the most impatient with myself. I admire leaders who have patience; it is not only a virtue, but a valuable skill you can use in negotiations and to win the hearts and minds of people.

Abraham Lincoln is one of history's best examples of patience. Constantly besieged by friends and foes alike, he remained patient and steadfast in his decision-making. Perhaps he was even patient to a fault when it came to replacing the sluggish and faltering Union generals in the first years of the Civil War.

One who tested Lincoln's patience too much was his first commanding general, George McClellan. A sarcastic President Lincoln wired General McClellan: "I have just read your dispatch about sore-tongued and fatigued horses. Will you pardon me for asking what the horses of your army have done since the battle of Antietam that fatigues anything?"

Lincoln was clearly out of patience with McClellan. The President had ordered him to pursue Confederate General Robert E. Lee into Virginia after Antietam on September 17, 1862, but McClellan dallied more than a month. A little over a week after sending this message, Lincoln replaced McClellan with Ambrose Burnside.

In the first year of his presidency, Lincoln had to fill numerous vacancies in the government. Filling each vacancy, he once remarked: " ... there are twenty applicants, and of these I must make nineteen enemies." Every leader who has had to make tough personnel decisions knows exactly what Lincoln is talking about.

Still, Lincoln handled these routine duties with uncommon patience and forbearance—while at the same time he was saving a nation.

My dad was a man of great patience. Once he and I had manhandled a large tire off the tractor and had it propped up precariously to load in the pickup. In my haste, I backed the pickup into the tire and knocked it flat to the ground. The tire weighed over two-hundred pounds and the day was very hot. Dad just looked at me and said, "Son, I wish you hadn't done that."

On many occasions, I am sure Terry Townsend, the man who brought me into association management in 1973, thought that I was his worst hiring mistake. Terry, however, was infinitely patient. The only time I know for sure that he wanted to kill me was late one night when we were traveling together on a political road trip to West Texas.

While he slept in the front seat, I was driving and hit a dip in the road too fast, launching Terry and sending his bald head into the roof. By the time he came back down, I hit a second dip and up he went again, cracking his head again. Why he didn't fire me on the spot remains a mystery. I don't have a lot of patience, but for what I do have, the credit goes to Terry.

✦✦✦✦✦✦

When you are patient with your people after they make mistakes or otherwise disappoint, you build a reservoir of trust and respect. A leader who demonstrates patience when everyone else is losing theirs not only gains esteem, but becomes the *go-to guy* when the next load hits the twirling blades.

A professional lobbyist either learns patience, leaves the profession, or is hauled away by men in white coats. It is not easy when you've had to sit for hours in a public hearing or waited outside a senator's door while he talks on the phone through your scheduled appointment time. It's even worse when you have an important bill being debated on the house or senate floor and you're confined to watching the gallery while others decide the future of your legislative agenda.

During one session, I asked a senator to sponsor a minor bill to clarify an existing regulation. The bill was not technical and the senator was known for his effectiveness, but he did imbibe from time to time. When he began to discuss the bill it was quite obvious he had had a liquid lunch because he mumbled into his microphone and no one could understand what he was saying.

One of his colleagues, who, as we say in West Texas, was a little slow on the draw, began asking questions. Neither had the foggiest idea what the other was talking about, and I was dying a slow death. Finally to my relief, the senator quit asking questions and the bill passed. My patience kept me out of the ICU for another day.

Patience is a valuable leadership skill. In negotiations, for example, if you are serving on a publicly elected board and the decision involves millions of taxpayer dollars, by being patient and remaining clear-headed, you can become the final arbiter of the matter.

Patience when dealing with emotional issues is a critical leadership competency, as anyone who has served on a school board can attest. An average school board meeting may attract a few concerned citizens; add a bond issue and the front rows fill up. Bring up any issue that affects kids and you'll be adding chairs in the auditorium ... and don't expect facts, reason, or logic to have a damn thing to do with the proceedings.

On one particular night, the auditorium was filled well before the board chair convened the meeting, and few had left by the time the ordeal ended past one in the morning. At issue was the selection criteria for the girls' dance team. In this instance, the dance director had decided one criterion would be the size of the girls' thighs. No, I am absolutely not making this up.

In what I later dubbed "The Great Thigh Debate," hours and hours of tearful testimony by moms, dads, and daughters tested the patience of every member of the board ... but as the saying goes, that's why we got paid the big bucks. In the end, we stayed the course, looked as serious as we could, and patiently endured the evening. Our ultimate decision: thigh measurements were out as a qualification to dance.

I remember thinking at some point during the evening that volunteering to serve on the school board made as much sense as a chicken volunteering to work for Colonel Sanders.

PERSEVERANCE & RESILIENCE

"You take a few falls and you learn to bounce back, it's all part of living in the aftermath."
–Bob Seger

"I'm gonna go down rockin' or I ain't going down at all."
–Waylon Jennings

Perseverance and Resilience are different sides of a two-headed coin. To persevere is to hold on to your purpose and principles despite setbacks, disappointments and armchair quarterbacking from the cheap seats.

Resilience is the ability to bounce back from defeats, recover from life's lumps.

Abraham Lincoln, Franklin Roosevelt, and Winston Churchill were three of the most persevering and resilient leaders in history; and certain character defects not withstanding, add Richard Nixon and Bill Clinton. Just when the country thought it had heard the last of Nixon and Clinton, back they would spring into our lives. The line from one of Bobby Vee's '60s hits: "Like a rubber ball, I'll come bouncing back to you ..." could be their theme song.

Eleanor Roosevelt was a woman of great conscience and character who, persisting against her husband's critics and small-minded people, pursued her goals of social, gender, and racial equality.

On September 7, 1960, in Rome, a young Wilma Rudolf became the first American woman to win three gold medals in the Olympics, despite being born into racial segregation and poverty. Contracting polio at the age of four, she was told she would never walk again. Wilma obviously proved them wrong and she also never gave up against the brain cancer that finally killed her at the age of fifty-four.

Thomas Edison experienced a thousand failures with the lightbulb before discovering the winner. Lincoln was defeated numerous times for public office before he won the White House. Perseverance has its own rewards.

++++++

We first met Pamela when my wife Sherry tutored her daughter in math. Pam, was struggling with family issues and, in her mid-forties, was also attending the University of Texas to get her bachelor's degree.

Since childhood she had learning difficulties that challenged her every day in the classroom. Many of her teachers were indifferent, unwilling, or simply lacked the training to help her; but she had a spirit that just didn't comprehend the word "no."

Pam persevered. From one personal set back to another, like that rubber ball, she came bouncing back.

In December, 2002, we attended Pam's UT graduation, where she was literally the first person to walk across the stage—because no one else wanted to go first. She received her Bachelor of Science Degree in Applied Learning and Development with a minor in Speech Communications. She wants to teach children with learning disabilities and encourage them to believe in themselves.

If gold medals were given for perseverance and resilience, this homemaker and mother of two would have a collection. Pam accomplished all of this, even though she is dyslexic.

✦✦✦✦✦✦

We all know a Pam who has been dealt a losing hand, but has had the tenacity and determination to become a winner. They do not think of themselves as heroes but, of course, they are. Their resilience inspires us; their perseverance challenges us to, in the words of Winston Churchill, "Never give up, never give up, never give up."

President Franklin D. Roosevelt was a model of resilience and perseverance. He overcame a crippling disease to be elected President for four terms and led this nation through some of its darkest days.

Tom Brokaw returned from his visit to Normandy on the fiftieth anniversary of D-Day and wrote about the greatest generation America has ever produced. In his runaway bestseller, *The Greatest Generation,* NBC Anchorman Brokaw recounts the stories of the men who fought on the beaches of Normandy in June 1944, as well as many of the men and women who served the country on the home front.

This generation, united by a common purpose and common values, also had in common an uncommon leader in President Roosevelt. FDR guided the nation for twelve years, including leading America through its two monumental crises of the 20th Century—the Great Depression and World War II. According to Pulitzer-Prize-winning biographer Doris Kearns Goodwin, "No factor was more important to Roosevelt's success than his confidence in himself and his unshakable belief in the American people."

It was this confidence that gave him the personal power to persist through the first year of the War, when American victories were few and far between.

At the time of President Roosevelt's death, *The New York Times* editorialized: "It was his leadership which inspired free men in every part of the world to fight with greater hope and courage." One of his severest political critics, Republican Senator Howard Taft, gave perhaps the greatest epitaph: "The President...dies a hero of the war, for he literally worked himself to death in the service of the American people."

On those days when we feel that we are "working ourselves to death," we would do well to pause and think of the enormous challenges President Roosevelt faced from 1933 until his death in 1945. His "greater hope and courage" can inspire us to persevere when the walls are closing in and the only news is bad news.

"Resilience," according to the American Psychological Association (APA), "is not a trait that people either have or do not have. It involves behaviors, thoughts, and actions that can be learned and developed in anyone." Bouncing back from difficult experiences is never a cake walk, but ordinary people do it all the time; no headlines, no blaring trumpets, no appearances on Oprah.

The APA offers the following factors associated with resilience:

- Having caring and supportive relationships both inside and outside the family
- A positive view of yourself and confidence in your strengths and abilities
- Skills in communication and problem solving
- The capacity to manage strong feelings and impulses
- The capacity to make realistic plans and take steps to carry them out.

PLANNING

"A plan is a list of actions arranged in whatever sequence is thought likely to achieve an objective."
                                        -John Argenti

"Whatever failures I have known, whatever errors I have committed, whatever follies I have witnessed in private and public life have been the consequence of action without thought."
                                        -Bernard Baruch

Minutes
Board of Directors
Association for the Preservation of the Status Quo
July 4, 2002

Item One

The executive director announced that even though the association had never had a lawsuit, the association should have a prestigious law firm on retainer, at the cost of $50,000 per year.

On motion, without discussion, the recommendation was unanimously approved.

Item Two

The Chairman of the Annual Conference Committee announced the location for next year's annual convention to be Tahiti; and because many of the board member's companies had suffered financial losses in the previous year, the association would pay their roundtrip airfare.

On motion, without discussion, the recommendation was unanimously approved.

Item Three

Since it had been 10 years since the last strategic-planning retreat, the executive director recommended that the board conduct a strategic-planning retreat with a professional facilitator.

On motion, after much discussion, the recommendation to fire the executive director was unanimously approved.

✦✦✦✦✦✦

Nothing brings a greater sense of panic to a board of directors than mention of the word *planning*. The word *deficit* comes close, but my money is still on the former. Like reacting to fingernails on a chalkboard, board members quickly cover their ears as they break dance to the exits.

Boards will retain attorneys, CPAs, and other professionals to solve their legal or business issues, but when it comes to investing time and money into planning for the future, they become a collection of Scrooges.

Boards will routinely (1) avoid planning like the plague, or (2) get by as cheaply as possible, or (3) insist it just isn't needed at this time—maybe next year, or the next, or (4) all of the above. Boards simply do not like to take the time or spend the money to plan. To be fair, this attitude is not totally without justification. There are myriad reasons why boards stop short of a professional planning effort: some members have been burned by inept planners in their own businesses or organizations; others have wasted thousands of dollars on a plan that sits collecting dust on the top shelf; still others hold the attitude that if they are not *doing*, they are wasting their time.

Effective leaders know that planning is critical to the viability of the organization. As Harvard Business School professor Michael Porter asserts: "If you want to make a difference as a leader, you've got to make time for strategy."

Boards of directors that do not take the time to plan strategically are succumbing to the advice given freely by Yogi Berra: "When you come to the fork in the road, take it." This may be fine if you are on an unscripted adventure, but not if you are a steward of your organization.

Strategic planning need not be expensive or painful; in fact it can be a source of satisfaction and enjoyment. A well-designed planning session can yield significant benefits to the organization at a reasonable cost and at an acceptable level of risk by:

- Permitting and encouraging the emergence of innovative programs
- Permitting and encouraging the identification of problems
- Introducing new ideas or new methods to approaching old problems
- Determining the value of current programs and services (making the sacred cows moo loudly)
- Increasing the ownership of the board members, volunteer leaders, donors, and staff
- Unifying the board on expectations and objectives
- Effectively allocating organizational resources (people and money)
- Keeping the organization focused on those priorities that result in the most value to members, constituents, stakeholders, and others

Perhaps leaders would be more inclined toward strategic planning if it were called another name, such as "preventing disaster," or "maintaining future Return On

Investment." But whatever you call it, organizations must adopt the Boy Scout motto "be prepared" to remain relevant in a rapidly changing and competitive world of rising constituent demands and expectations.

To be blunt, a board of a nonprofit organization that doesn't engage in strategic planning at least every three years is not acting in the best interests of its membership. And the shame, distressingly, is that the planning process can be both energizing and, yes, fun. It does take time and money, but the investment is minimal compared to the benefits it brings to the organization.

A seasoned pilot never lifts his wheels without submitting a detailed flight plan. John Wooden, who built the greatest college basketball dynasty in history at UCLA, didn't just show up ten minutes before the big game and tell his players, "Okay guys, go out there and win one for the Gipper," leaving the team wondering just who in the hell is the Gipper? A skilled surgeon doesn't just open his patient up and then exclaim, "Now which one of these buggers are we supposed to remove?"

General Dwight David Eisenhower, presiding over one of the most detailed military plans in world history, the D-Day invasion of Normandy, said, "Rely on planning, but don't trust the plan." Planning is a process, not a one-time event.

Strategic planning is another board responsibility that cannot be delegated, although it can and should be shared with the senior staff of the organization. Planning is an act, but must also be construed as an ongoing action. In fact, the development of action plans for each objective—by assigning responsibilities and resources to each objective—is always in a dynamic, not static, state of existence. The plan must also allow for flexibility to respond to changes in the organization's environment, both internal and external; as well as the inevitable surprises, both good and bad.

Why do plans fail? Here are some of the reasons:

- Done for the wrong reasons
- Poor planning design
- Unrealistic expectations
- Trying to do too much
- Lacks leadership buy-in
- No accountability
- Staff and leadership not committed
- Insufficient resources committed for process
- Projections too far into the future
- Goals and objectives not linked to mission
- Inflexible—unresponsive to changes in the environment
- Plan not linked to financial plan/association resources
- Not properly communicated to membership
- Not understanding it is both a product and a process
- No follow-up or measurement

To reiterate, planning can be fun. The planning session is an opportunity to stretch beyond the obvious, beyond the "this is the way we've always done it" mentality. Planning becomes tedious or boring only when it has no structure or the board refuses to commit the time, money, and energy required.

A board leader must be an advocate for a professional planning process. I don't think it is hyperbole to say that next to caring for your professional staff, sound planning is the best investment an organization can make to control its own destiny.

RECONCILIATION

"We must learn to live together as brothers or perish together as fools."
    –Martin Luther King Jr.

"Every action done in company, ought to be with some sign of respect to those that are present."
    –George Washington

When two or more are gathered, the potential for conflict exists. Critical thinking and rigorous debate can lead to conflict within a board of directors. The good news is this can bring out new ideas, new solutions for old problems and bring new strategies into focus. Boards may discover there is more than one right answer to a seemingly irresolvable problem.

The bad news is that conflict can also lead to divisiveness or discord, and if not dealt with quickly and fairly, can lead to dysfunction and damaging consequences for the organization. Before a board splits into two armed camps, however, it needs to remember who it is working for—who it is accountable to. Board members simply do not have the luxury of divided loyalties when their overriding loyalty must be to their stakeholders.

"That a conflict should rage openly," John Gardner writes, "and damage the joint enterprise is not the only bad outcome. It can go underground, remain unresolved, and do even more damage. The sounds of bickering are part of the necessary noisiness of a free society; but ... beyond a certain point ... confrontation becomes counterproductive."

Ron Kessler, an attorney with 35 years of legal experience, states there are six sources of potential conflict:

1. Different perceptions of same issue or problem;
2. Rub between different personalities, temperament, cultural or heritage;
3. Dissimilar core values;
4. Outright misunderstandings, unresolved bitterness or offenses, unmet needs;
5. Insecurities, poor self image, competition, perceived threats;
6. Disagreement/misunderstanding on purpose, vision, goals, methods or values.

I can tell you from personal experience that Ron has identified the key elements of conflict. After 21 years with an organization, I became involved in a professional conflict that contained all six elements and did not have a happy ending.

In my final year as president of the Texas Motor Transportation Association, I witnessed how the inability to reconcile differences led, in the words of John Gardner, to conflict that "raged openly" and later forced the divisiveness "underground." This led to harmful decisions that did unnecessary damage to the organization.

The trucking industry was evolving from a tightly government-regulated industry into a deregulated one, and the increasing competition between our member companies had erupted into charges and countercharges about who had the industry's best interests at heart. Motives were questioned, different perceptions of opportunities and threats drove previously long-time friends apart, and misunderstandings turned into mistrust. The board chair, following the old General Motors philosophy, believed that what was good for his company was good for the industry. Case closed.

Policy disputes can quickly become distorted by personalities unless the leadership takes a proactive role to mediate and resolve the differences. Once the debate deteriorates into personal attacks, it is hard to reverse the descent into the bottomless pit of derision and unresolved bitterness.

This inability, and to some degree, unwillingness, to resolve the association's core issues, led to my resignation and to a major split within the ranks of the membership. It was several years before a new CEO and new leadership were able to repair some of the damage. Even today, it is not the first-tier organization that it had been for over 50 years.

As a leader, you may not be able to resolve a conflict by yourself, but by recognizing the symptoms and knowing some basic ideas about conflict resolution, you may be able to prevent permanent damage. Apply these practical ideas from Ron Kessler:

1. Approach the problem as soon as possible; take time to have a face-to-face meeting.
2. Focus solely on the issue of conflict.
3. Generate valid and useful information.
4. Give people permission to disagree.
5. Allow people the power to state their position.
6. Protect people from being needlessly hurt.
7. Suggest options to creatively solve conflict.
8. Allow some time to pass after the intervention.
9. Stay committed to the relationship.

Add number 10:

10. See number 2.

This is crucial. Always keep the focus on the issue of conflict and avoid personalizing the issue at all costs. Policy differences seldom lead to lingering bitterness; personal attacks guarantee it.

Reconciliation is the act of reestablishing a close relationship. If conflict does occur, leaders must be adept at resolving conflict and then be able to take the next essential step to reconcile the parties. Each member of the board has the personal responsibility to push the personalities aside and focus on achieving the mission of the organization.

If conflict creates hurt feelings and your efforts at reconciliation keep falling short, take heart and keep persisting. I can think of at least one conflict in our nation's history where most of those directly involved would never have believed there could be reconciliation.

There have been few acts of healing as noble and high-minded as that which occurred at Appomattox Court House in Virginia on April 9, 1865. The nation had just concluded four years of bitterness and bloodshed when General Robert E. Lee, Commander of the Army of Northern Virginia, surrendered to the leader of the Union Armies, General Ulysses S. Grant.

Because of the deep bitterness the war had brought to both sides, the South was prepared for the worst. But those who had been underestimating Grant throughout the war underestimated him again. He was determined to preserve the dignity of the valiant Confederate soldiers and had his men show genuine respect to their defeated foes. General Lee was so taken by Grant's generosity of spirit at the surrender that after the war he would not allow a harsh word about Grant to be said in his presence.

If Lee and Grant could reconcile so graciously after trying for four long years to destroy each other, surely you can persist and continue to affirm the value and dignity of each individual involved.

In any volunteer organization, particularly those whose members have been elected by the community, the potential for conflict over issues will always exist. Healthy dissent is not bad for the organization; in fact it can lead to new ideas, innovation, and needed change. But when the disagreement becomes petty and personal, it is not just the individuals who lose, but the organization and the constituents as well.

As a dedicated volunteer leader, you should fight the fight to the best of your ability as long as you do so ethically. If your side wins, be a gracious winner. If you lose, be a gracious loser and join with the majority of the board in carrying out the new policy or initiative. If you disagree so strongly, you may continue to press your case within the parameters of accepted protocol. If you remain so opposed, however, that your disagreement leads you to destructive attempts to win your case, you should resign in the best interests of the organization.

The politics of polarization can render any board of directors, elected or volunteer, helpless when it comes to the achievement of the mission. Choose your fights carefully; be prepared to win some and lose some. And in the end if you truly can't say, "Would you like for me to make it unanimous?" then you may need to take a close look inside yourself to see if you are going to be able to support the group's decision. If you can't, perhaps you should move on. Reconciling differences, like showing humility, is not an act of weakness; it is an act of leadership, one that will make you better able to meet new challenges.

RISK-TAKING

"If you always do what you've always done, then you will always get what you've always gotten."
—John Maxwell

"Be nice, feel guilty, and play safe. If there was ever a prescription for producing a dismal future, that has to be it."
—Walter Wriston

Approaching the edge of the high diving board, the youngster cautiously moves toward his first high dive. Peering over the board, he looks into the water below, shudders and hesitates.

Regaining his confidence, he concentrates on what he has learned and, with his adrenaline in overdrive, soars into the pool below. He pops out of the water to the cheers of his coach and friends. The risk was truly worth the price.

Running to be the first in the water, the daredevil reaches the weathered rope first and swings out over the old swimming hole. As he releases the rope with the smile of victory on his lips, he looks down and sees that the creek is dry!

Waking up in a body cast at the local hospital, he thinks to himself, "Next time I had better look before I leap!"

✦✦✦✦✦✦

A prudent, calculated risk may not always succeed; nor does a lack of planning guarantee failure. But the odds favor the far-sighted strategy over the ready-shoot-aim approach.

Most boards are not just risk-adverse; they will avoid taking any risk whatsoever. In fact, paranoia may not be too strong a description. But a board that clings to the status quo and rejects any risk-taking meant to improve the quality of services in a rapidly changing environment needs multiple doses of reality.

"But if we take a risk, we might fail and look stupid." Don't worry, if you haven't risked abandoning a nonworking program, dismantling a governance structure first adopted in the Middle Ages, or implementing a new marketing strategy for dealing with a changing constituency, you already *are* stupid.

✦✦✦✦✦✦

In the first years of the Civil War, before the major Union victory at Gettysburg, the Confederate Army under the command of Robert E. Lee had consistently beat the Federal armies with alarming success. One of the key reasons lay in Lee's willingness to take bold risks.

On May 2, 1863, during the Battle of Chancellorsville, Lee took a huge gamble by splitting his troops and sending the bulk of his force, commanded by General Stonewall Jackson, on a daring flanking maneuver that brought a key Confederate victory. The risk was enormous and had General Jackson not been successful, Lee would have experienced a major—and maybe decisive—defeat.

On the surface, it may appear that Lee risked too much on this one battle. A closer look, however, reveals that while he took a significant risk, it was a calculated one.

In sending Jackson on the flanking maneuver, Lee had calculated the following: First, he knew that the Union Commander John Hooker was an overly cautious leader, despite his nickname, "Fighting Joe." Since Hooker had only recently taken command of the Union army, Lee believed his opponent would not risk a major defeat by making an aggressive move.

Second, it had been only a few months since the crushing defeat of the Union army at Fredericksburg. Lee again calculated that a surprise move would catch the Federals off guard because he knew they were tired and were suffering from low morale. Third, Lee had great confidence in Stonewall Jackson, who had proved in numerous battles to be an aggressive fighter.

It was a risk, but one he made with knowledge and research. Lee believed the risk was worth the price; he made his calculated decision and it paid off. The bitter irony of Lee's victory at Chancellorsville was the unfortunate death of Stonewall Jackson. Jackson was mortally wounded by his own troops who, on a dark night, mistakenly took him for the enemy.

+ + + + + +

By their nature, boards don't like to cut programs and services; they like to add them. But abandonment is essential to innovation in an environment of scarce resources. With increasing pressures of time, less money, more competition, and diversity, associations must be prepared to take risks to reallocate resources from worn-out programs to those with current value.

As British management consultant Charles Handy writes, "It is one of the paradoxes of success that the things and the ways which got you where you are, are seldom those that keep you there. ... To continue to be successful in a period of accelerating change and uncertainty, we will have to change, fundamentally, the way we are working now."

If you accept Handy's argument that change is not an option in a constantly-changing world, then the decision to stay where you are is a riskier course of action than the alternative. By doing your homework, collecting the right data, and developing a solid consensus, you will mitigate the risk factors and be able to dive into the future with confidence. You will never eliminate all of the risk in a major-change initiative, but as a wise sage once said, "the status ain't quo no mo!"

✦✦✦✦✦✦

"If a strong board," writes Robert Greenleaf, "sets distinction as its goal, invests the time and energy, organizes itself for the task, and stays with it, distinction is practically assured. The place to start is with an unequivocal trustee obligation to deliver a new, more serving institution."

Risk does not have to be just another four-letter word when undertaken with prudence, diligence, and foresight. Do not be afraid to take a risk; *be afraid not to.* As a board, consider the following questions as a prelude for strategic planning and prudent risk-taking:

1. What assumptions can be made about the future environment of our industry, profession, constituency group, or issue arena?

2. What one or two realistic innovations or occurrences, not possible today, would fundamentally change our industry, profession, or constituency?

3. Where do those you serve want to go that they haven't even thought about?

4. Based on your expectations for the foreseeable future, what should you as a leader consider doing to respond to a need, opportunity, or condition that you might create for your stakeholders?

5. What will happen to our organization or community if we do not take action on this specific change initiative during the coming year?

SERVANT LEADERSHIP

"The most important qualification for trustees should be that they care for the institution, which means that they care for all the people the institution touches, and that they are determined to make their caring count."
                                        –Robert Greenleaf

"The first responsibility of a leader is to define reality. The last is to say thank you. In between the two, the leader must become a servant and a debtor ..."
                                        –Max De Pree

In 1986, as a member of the building committee for the Texas Society of Association Executives, I took pride watching then Governor Mark White break ground on this exciting new venture for our society of professional association executives. Ten years later, as the newly selected president and Chief Staff Officer, I recommended to the board of directors that the society sell the building to offset financial losses, the cost of building maintenance, and to help finance the development of new programs and services to the membership.

During the ten years between the open house and the recommendation to sell, the building had been subject to the

wild gyrations of the Austin real-estate market. When the
building was fully leased it was a financial asset, but all too
often the vagaries of the market had the association staff and
leadership scrambling to meet our debts and overcome
rental-income shortfalls.

In 1996, shortly after I became president the largest
tenant moved out, leaving the association with an annual
hickey of approximately $100,000. The decision to sell the
building was not taken lightly; the building had been a
source of prestige and recognition for the society and had
the added advantage of location, location, location.

We did our due diligence and in the end, the board
voted to place the building up for sale. There was only one
dissenting vote, Vice Chair Brad Duggan, CAE. Throughout
the building deliberation, Brad, whose wife is a successful
real-estate broker, argued the case for holding on to the
building as the association's only real hard asset. His arguments were reasoned and thoughtful, but the majority eventually prevailed.

Immediately after the vote, Brad turned to me and
said, "Would you like for me to make it unanimous? The
decision has been made and I will do everything I can to help
make this sale a success." And he did.

Brad's gracious act was servant leadership at its best.
Not once did he complain or criticize other members of the
board or the staff. He was the essence of a team player.

The irony of this story is that over the course of the
next year we "sold" the building at least three different
times, but did not actually close on the sale for over a year. By
the time money actually changed hands, Brad was chair.
There is no question that had Brad been a vindictive person
or had he had a personal agenda, he could have disrupted
the sale. As board chair, he could have used his power to sway
other members of the board.

It never crossed his mind. The consummate servant
leader had been true to his word by working hard to make

the sale a success. Once the decision was made, Brad fully supported the will of the majority.

✦✦✦✦✦✦

As a CEO of two different organizations, I have been blessed with several terrific servant leaders. One of my all-time favorite people is Sam Bishop, a trucking company executive, who served as Board Chair of TMTA in the early 90s. Sam has a great sense of humor, but also the ability to cut to the chase.

During his year as chair, we not only had to deal with a legislative session; we were also going through a merger with another organization. If you have ever experienced the thrill of merging two organizations, you know it requires an enormous amount of time and energy while you keep an intense focus on each and every detail. Throw in a legislative session on top of that, and you have a recipe for what the Rolling Stones best described as a "nineteenth nervous breakdown."

Sam took it all in stride. His steady demeanor kept the wheels from falling off on many close calls; but more important was his complete devotion to the best interests of the association and its members. The association's agenda was Sam's, and vice versa.

When the association board approved supporting a bill in the legislature that offered no help to his company and in fact would help his competitors, Sam never used the power of his gavel. There's no question he could have blocked approval, but I don't think it ever crossed his mind.

Sam believed it was in the best overall interest of the association to support the bill, and he was not going to inject a personal agenda into the organization for which he cared so much. It would be only a couple of years later that I fully understood how much that meant to a volunteer organization. (See Reconciliation.)

Sam was oblivious to power and prestige. He never once lost sight of for whom he worked. He knew that when he accepted the gavel at the annual convention, he was accountable first and foremost to the members of the association, even at the expense of his own company. Sam will always be one of my heroes.

Servant Leadership is putting the goals of the organization, and the needs of the people responsible for attaining those goals, first; and making sure that all impediments and obstacles to reaching those goals are removed. The true servant leader does this without thought to personal agendas, or other ego-related issues ... this may be difficult at times, but it is essential to the well-being, and, therefore, the ultimate success, of the organization itself.

STEWARDSHIP & PARTNERSHIP

"The only gift is a portion of thyself."
–Ralph Waldo Emerson

"Everybody can be great because everybody can serve. You only need a heart full of grace, a soul generated by love."
–Martin Luther King, Jr.

If the horrific events of 9/11 were not enough to test the character of our country, the smoke was still rising from the fallen twin towers when corporate scandals fouled our nation's air in the fall of 2001. Although the fallout from the corporate misdeeds makes an inadequate comparison to 9/11, this was yet another terrible tragedy that caused the loss of thousands of jobs and many millions of dollars in savings and retirement income.

As I mentioned in the Introduction, a pressing question that the Enron disaster and later scandals revealed is: "Where was the board of directors when corporate management was destroying the company?" The board has a powerful role in any organization, for-profit or nonprofit, and is the one entity charged with the most accountability— to the stakeholders, constituents, or members.

Accountability is the heart of effective governance; effective governance gives the organization strength and stability. On the other hand, stewardship is the conscience of the organization. "Conscience" is defined as the moral goodness or blameworthiness of one's own conduct, intentions, or character, together with a feeling of obligation to do right or be good.

Where was the blameworthiness or the feeling of obligation to do right or be good when the Enron board was allowing the company's stakeholders and employees to be robbed of their careers and life savings? Stewardship is a 24/7 obligation to the organization's constituents. Where was the board?

This example of board irresponsibility underscores the sacred responsibility that a board of directors has to its constituents, stakeholders, donors, and members. While most nonprofit and community board members are devoted to the cause or mission, many never fully appreciate the role they share *as a board* for the stewardship of the enterprise.

Effective stewardship not only implies strict accountability to the constituents, it also requires the sharing of power or responsibilities between the players. On a superbly functioning board of directors, stewardship is marked by the interdependence and collaboration of the trustees. Stewardship and partnership may not be synonymous; they are, however, inextricably linked. In *Stewardship: Choosing Service Over Self-Interest*, Peter Block identifies four requirements for partnership:

1. Partnership means everyone has a voice in defining the purpose, goals, objectives, and acceptable outcomes for the organization.

2. Partners have the right to say no. A partner may lose an argument or a vote, but never his voice.

3. Partners share joint accountability for the success and/or failure of the endeavor.

4. Partners must be absolutely honest with one another.

The link between partnership and stewardship provides great insight for understanding how boards can operate more effectively. Merriam-Webster describes a partnership as "a relationship usually involving close cooperation between parties having specified joint rights and responsibilities." This is an accurate description of how a board partnership is intended to work.

"Partnerships work," writes Russ Moxley, "when power is shared ... it is not a partnership when one person or several people have power and others don't." Partners have a shared sense of purpose; while their tactics and strategies may differ, they are united by a strong sense of direction for the organization.

In addition, "partnership begins with a deep respect for the person; it is based on a deep-down-in-the-gut belief in the worth and value of every person." This is the essence of any successful organization or venture; people matter more than anything else.

When you find an organization, for-profit or nonprofit, that has as its core belief the dignity of each individual, the odds are overwhelming you have found an organization that sustains results. Stretching this point, I would argue that it is the essential ingredient in a volunteer organization.

Scrolling down the list of definitions for "partner," you will eventually come to this: "one of the heavy timbers that strengthen a ship's deck to support a mast—usually used in plural." Wow! What a great metaphor for the relationship between individuals serving on a board.

Each timber must be firmly in place to support the mast; take away one and the mast becomes unstable. When the sailing is smooth, there may be no problem, but when the ship hits rough seas, the voyage is in peril.

You've probably never considered yourself to be "one of the heavy timbers supporting the mast" of your organization, but that is exactly what you are. Your individual strength is magnified when combined with the other "timbers" in a partnership of shared responsibility and accountability.

++++++

While this is not a book about the legal responsibilities of a board, the following story is a serious reminder that a board leader must never let a moment's lapse of judgment put the organization at risk.

At TMTA, we usually had one board meeting a year away from Austin. Following the afternoon board meeting, we held a reception and dinner. One morning during such an out-of-town meeting, I was approached by two female members of our staff, a senior staff member and an assistant. The night before, the young and attractive assistant had been riding the elevator to her floor when a board member with too much to drink made a sexual innuendo.

The assistant brushed him off and he made no further moves. The young woman, while rightfully offended, was not inclined to take any action, but did want me to know about it. I asked her if she would be satisfied with a letter of apology and she said yes.

While I did not believe that she might later change her mind, I knew it was my responsibility to attempt to limit any potential liability to the association. I quietly approached the board member who first denied the incident happened.

I told him that if he denied it and she stuck to her story, I would have no alternative but to go to the Executive Committee. Any accusation of sexual harassment by a staff member toward a member of the board could place the whole association at risk. I also suggested that if the young woman were to receive a written, personal apology, the incident would be forgotten.

I knew a couple of things going into the meeting with the board member. One, he was married; and two, he was in a middle-management position in his company. A nice guy, he had let a weak moment place both his career and the association at risk, to say nothing of his marriage. Within an hour of our conversation, the board member discreetly handed me an envelope and I passed his apology on to the assistant.

I share this story, not because it happens frequently in volunteer organizations; it is actually the rare exception. I share it because a board member must never let his guard down in any manner that would jeopardize the organization. Stewardship never takes a sabbatical.

✦✦✦✦✦✦

Board stewards have an additional role to play in the community at large. Stewards of the organization or community are like servant leaders. They serve society, not themselves.

An authentic leader stresses the organization's responsibility to the surrounding society. Leaders must have a broad perspective, realizing that the organization cannot be an island of self-interest. It must interact and support the larger community. Robert Greenleaf, author of *Servant Leadership*, says it very well: "Caring for persons, the more able and the less able serving each other, is the rock upon which a good society is built."

The Board of Trustees of the School District has the primary responsibility of ensuring a public school education of the highest standards for the students and parents who reside in the district. But it also has the obligation to be a good citizen of the community, working with both private and public entities to enhance the overall quality of living in the community.

Likewise a trade association that represents the special interests of its members does not operate in a vacuum. It also has the obligation to give something back to the community.

Too often, this concept of stewardship meets resistance from a board of directors too focused on its own narrow concerns. It is up to the enlightened leaders in the organization to persuade the board it is not only the ethical thing to do, but in their best business and political interests as well.

For example, The Houston Automobile Dealers' Association (HADA) founded EARNING BY LEARNING OF HOUSTON. This program, created in 1991, serves as a role-model program hailed by teachers, administrators, and fourth graders throughout the Houston Independent School District.

The program is simple. At-risk fourth graders in the H.I.S.D. are paid one dollar for every book read and reported on to a teacher or volunteer. The program has expanded to 122 elementary schools with 6,500 students reading over 100,000 books annually. Also, largely due to the success of the Houston program, five other Texas cities have formed EARNING BY LEARNING programs. According to the teachers participating in the program, the children's vocabulary and communication skills have greatly improved.

In 1993, out of 504 entries, the HADA received the National Summit Award from the American Society of Association Executives. Although the program has received widespread acclaim from national associations and local elected officials, it is the heartwarming letters from the children that provide the most satisfaction and pride to the car dealers.

SUSTAINED RESULTS

"The leader's job is to make sure the right results are being achieved, the right things are being done."

–Peter Drucker

"There is no traffic jam on the second mile."

–John Maxwell

"The first virtue of a solider is the discipline of endurance."

–Napoleon

"I'm gonna give my only suit to The Salvation Army and everything else I'll leave behind ..." laments country singer Johnny Cash as he says farewell to a love-gone-bad in the soulful ballad "Don't Think Twice, It's All Right." Johnny might be consoled, however, that he was donating his suit to "by far the most effective organization in the U.S.," according to management expert Peter Drucker.

Not the most effective *nonprofit* organization, but the most effective organization in the United States, period. Although the Salvation Army is visible to most of us between Thanksgiving and Christmas, "no one even comes close to it with respect to clarity of mission, ability to innovate, measurable results, dedication, and putting money to maximum use."

Drucker has this warning for nonprofit organizations: "Performance is the ultimate test of any institution." Over the years, nonprofits have often tried to justify their existence by doing good deeds, without placing an emphasis on organizational performance.

No more. Donors, constituents, and even public officials are demanding that a nonprofit not only *do good*, but *be good* by demonstrating measurable results. Good will is not enough.

To achieve results that meet the constant demands and changing expectations of the stakeholders is a real challenge for leaders in all organizations, at all levels, at all times. Producing sustained results year after year is the mark of exceptional leadership and organizational excellence. And as Drucker makes clear: "Results are achieved by concentrating, not splintering. That enormous organization, The Salvation Army, concentrates on only four or five programs. Its executives have the courage to say: 'This is not where we can make the greatest contribution. It does not really fit the strength we have.'"

"The best leaders," says Jim Collins, "are resolved to do whatever it takes to make the company great, no matter how big or hard the decisions." Individual leaders who resolve to "do whatever it takes" and who collaborate with like-minded peers are capable of creating extraordinary results for the organization or community of interests.

✦✦✦✦✦✦

As I write this chapter, the stock market continues to resemble the readout of an electrocardiogram. The standard joke is my 401(k) is now a 101(k).

But even before the 9/11 tragedy, one industry had achieved a reputation best described by terms such as bailout, bankruptcy, and big egos. One industry where it would be hard, if not impossible, to discover a record of sustainable results (positive, that is), would be the airline industry—with one major exception.

I first met Herb Kelleher, the now-retired, always outgoing, and, some might say, outrageous president of Southwest Airlines in the spring of 1975 during the session of the Texas Legislature. Herb and the current president of Southwest, Colleen Barrett, were lobbying the legislature to pass a bill that would allow the company to operate in Texas before the days of airline deregulation.

I especially remember three things about Herb, who *Texas Monthly* magazine once described as the "Energizer Bunny of the skies." We shared many laborious legislative committee hearings, often into the wee hours of the morning.

First, he has a wonderful sense of humor; he is a terrifically funny man. Second, he didn't have one pretentious bone in his body. Third, there was absolutely no missing his intense focus and fierce resolve to achieve his objective.

When Herb finally stepped down as the President and CEO of Southwest Airlines, his record of sustainable profits was unmatched in the industry. Herb told his people to "think small and act small and we'll get bigger. Think big and act like you're big shots and we'll get smaller."

Southwest has been recognized as one of the best companies to work for in America. There are many reasons for this, but one stands out and best reflects Herb's leadership philosophy: "Focus on individuals and capabilities, not titles. Deal with people, not positions."

When all the major airlines laid off people during the many downturns of the airline industry, Southwest tightened its belt, kept its focus, but more importantly, retained all its employees. Herb sustained results by sustaining people. If you've ever flown Southwest, you know what I'm talking about.

✦✦✦✦✦✦

If you enjoy philosophical arguments, how about this one: In business, sports, politics, or leadership, is it harder to get to the top, or harder to stay on top? I've heard it passionately argued both ways, but I side with the latter. Herb Kelleher and Southwest Airlines' climb to the top was filed with obstacles, but the ability to sustain their position at a much higher altitude than their competitors, year after year, is for me the greater accomplishment.

A trade association successful in supporting a bill critical to the industry makes a significant contribution to the well-being of its membership; but when the same organization can sustain a series of victories one legislative session after another, its members reward it with unquestioned loyalty.

A nonprofit organization that holds a record-breaking fundraising event wins the appreciation of its beneficiaries. If it is successful, year in and year out, in making worthwhile contributions to those in need, it earns the admiration of the entire community.

A school board that wins the passage of a needed bond issue is demonstrating noteworthy leadership. When honor-roll numbers rise and drop-out rates fall one school year to the next, the sustained results clearly indicate a flourishing partnership between the board, school administrators, and teachers.

The lesson for board leaders is this: You must continue to hone your skills—planning, judgment, decision-making, foresight, collaboration—and be constantly aware of changes in your internal and external environment. Pay attention to the details, both large and small—remember the Lone Ranger and Tonto (Foresight - page 65). Ask probing questions, test your ideas, and don't be afraid to take prudent, calculated risks.

Finally, remember you are in a partnership—a partnership with your fellow board members and with the professional staff. In the game of football, the quarterback is generally given too much of the credit when the team wins and too much of the blame when it loses. It takes a team to achieve the desired results and an even better one to sustain them. "We are all," observed Luciano De Crescenzo, "angels with only one wing; we can only fly while embracing each other."

✦✦✦✦✦✦

A paradox, however, on the road to sustaining results is when the organization tries to do too much and loses sight of its core purpose or mission. As the organization attempts to accomplish more and more, the end result is to actually provide less and less value to its constituents and stake-holders. Or as a lawyer friend once told me after losing thousands of dollars in real-estate investments, "If I had just stuck to the legal business, I would have saved myself a great deal of grief."

I encounter this "more is better" syndrome in virtually every planning session I facilitate. There are several reasons for this. First, the organization is honestly trying to find new ways to serve its constituents. Second, a key leader may aggressively promote a program they feel strongly about. Third, as mentioned previously, boards are not predisposed to abandoning any program even if only a few stakeholders are participating.

As a consequence, the organization's resources become stretched too thin to support all of the various programs, and it is unable to sustain results in its core areas. It is like pouring a glass of water from a pitcher and continuing to pour even though the contents are spilling all over the floor.

In planning sessions, my goal is to persuade the leadership to identify no more than three to five priorities where they can concentrate their resources to produce the most value for the constituents. This priority-focus is the most potent force toward achieving organizational success.

Stakeholder needs will almost always overshadow resources, but to recall the wisdom of The Salvation Army, "Need alone does not justify our moving in. We must match our strength, our mission, our concentration, our value." Matching the organization's strengths to it core values and mission is paramount.

Focus on value for your stakeholders. Peter Drucker encourages a board to ask these questions:

- Knowing what we know now, would we really start this program or service today?
- If this program or service is readily available elsewhere, why are we offering it?
- If we devoted our financial and human resources to another activity, would our constituents be better served?
- Is there a strategic and valid reason for subsidizing this activity?
- Will we still be offering this program or service in 3-5 years?
- Do we allocate all costs to the program or service? If we did, how likely would we be willing to continue it?

The last word on achieving sustainable results: When was the last time you and your fellow board members, in the interest of increasing member value, poked a few sacred cows until they bellowed?

TEAMWORK

> *"It makes no difference if we're talking about individual or organizational leadership. The principles are universal, not situation specific. Whether we're leading in governments, companies or nonprofits, the message is clear; we have to work together in order to achieve the greater good."*
>
> –Stephen Covey

> *"None of us is as smart as all of us."*
>
> –Warren Bennis

> *"We need to remember that we can do little alone and much together."*
>
> –Francis Hesslebein

I will admit I am a fan of both Sylvester Stallone and Steven Seagal, and their one-man-to-the-rescue characters. But outside of Hollywood, the rugged individualist, the man on the white horse, and the self-made man are a vanishing species, a dying breed—if they ever existed at all. They have met their final match in the growing complexity, competitiveness, and technological advances in the marketplace of ideas and innovation. The conductor may direct the orchestra, but it is the blending of the individual sounds that produces the masterpiece.

"There is a certain kind of leader," write Warren Bennis and Patricia Ward Biederman, who recruits only people like himself or herself. There is another, better kind of leader who realizes you can only accomplish extraordinary things by involving excellent people who can do things that you cannot."

According to Bennis and Biederman, "Great Groups" offer a leadership model where the leader and the team are able to achieve something together that neither could achieve alone. "The Leader finds greatness in the group. And he or she helps the members find it in themselves."

Great groups have these characteristics:

- They all have extraordinary leaders who have a keen eye for talent and who inspire trust and deserve it.

- They are composed of excellent individuals with the ability to work well with others.

- They are curious minds with a sense of urgency to find "creative boundary-busting solutions" rather than simplistic ones.

- They are passionate about what they are doing and are people who get things done.

- They have leaders who encourage, enable, and create an atmosphere in which people feel safe to fail.

✦✦✦✦✦✦

The tribute was a complete surprise. The staff and Board of the Texas Motor Transportation Association honored me for 20 years of service with a reception, following our directors' meeting at the Capitol Marriott Hotel in Austin, Texas.

Friends, neighbors, former staff members, professional associates, and elected officials had been invited, including a special friend, then Governor of Texas Ann

Richards. The Governor and others spoke and, frankly, lavished me with a great deal of praise. Members and colleagues congratulated me. With all of the positive comments about accomplishments and battles won, and with the help of a glass of wine or two, my head had gained several hat sizes by evening's end.

As I was talking with a group, one of the elder statesmen of the association entered the conversation by poking a finger in my chest. Cy Weller of San Antonio was one of my favorite board members. Then in his late seventies or early eighties, Cy seemed ageless, his mind as razor-sharp as ever. Cy and his brother Edgar had built a major trucking company from scratch. In fact, he and his brother were both attorneys. They started their practice with Edgar meeting clients in the front office; while, in the back room, Cy conducted all-night poker games to finance their practice.

As Cy poked at my chest, he said, "Do you know why you've been successful?" I was pretty full of myself so I puffed up a little more waiting for Cy to tell me "How Great Thou Art."

"Because," he said, "you are not a star!"

Poof. The deflation was immediate. Head size back to normal. Then I realized this wise business leader had paid me the evening's most valuable compliment. Of all the words of praise I received that evening almost 10 years ago, Cy's comment was the only one I remember—and will never forget.

Cy was right. I'm not a star; never have been, never will be. The success I have achieved in my career has always directly related to the people who have worked with me. To my credit, I have a knack for surrounding myself with the right people and creating successful teams to achieve goals and objectives.

I'm not without an ego, as I'm sure many of my former team members would quickly agree. But I learned early in my career from watching mentors like Terry Townsend, Mickey Moore, and Jim Taylor, who surrounded themselves with talented people and always emphasized teamwork and collaboration, that, as Warren Bennis writes, "None of us is as good as all of us."

Too many "leaders" have what *Good to Great* author Jim Collins calls the *biggest dog* syndrome—they don't mind other dogs in the kennel, as long as they remain the biggest one. These are the same leaders whose favorite word is *I*. They come in with trumpets blaring with "Hail to the Chief" ringing in their ears. Collins writes: "They look in the mirror to take credit for success, but out the window to assign blame for disappointing results."

At times when my vaccination for the biggest dog syndrome would wear off, I fortunately had team members who weren't afraid to tell me to sit and stay. Deborah Swift, my number two at the Texas Motor Transportation Association, and later Jill Weir, at the Texas Society of Association Executives, both excelled at telling me when I was barking too loudly and needed to go back and sit on the porch. Deborah would in no uncertain terms jerk my chain until I came to my senses, and Jill, twenty-plus years my junior and standing all of five feet tall, would simply tell me that I was full of it.

✦✦✦✦✦✦

Leadership, is never a solo act. In 1987, the Chicago Bulls' Michael Jordan won every honor imaginable, including Most Valuable Player, All-NBA first team, Defensive Player of the Year, All Star Game MVP, and the Slam Dunk Championship. But no NBA Championship! Jordan's teammates, wrote former Bulls' coach Phil Jackson, were like a supporting cast who were so enthralled by what he could do with a basketball that they never learned to work together successfully as a team.

From 1987 until that first Championship ring in 1991, both Jordan and his teammates came to realize that it is not brilliant individual performances that make great teams, but the energy unleashed when players put their egos aside and work toward a common goal. By the end of 1993, Jordan and the Bulls were shooting through the playoffs enroute to their third straight NBA Championship.

Good teams, Jackson observed, become great ones when members trust each other enough to surrender *me* for the *we* That *we* for the Chicago Bulls brought three NBA Championships in a row and a total of five in the 1990s. The team had learned that to win consistently, the individuals involved must surrender their self-interest for the greater good.

A board of directors can be an excellent template for the observation of effective teamwork. Of course, some boards are the last place to look for a model of teamwork and leadership. But the opportunity is always there.

Almost always, boards are composed of people with impressive resumes listing a wide set of individual skills and abilities. The challenge is to foster an environment where these individual talents can be combined to create one *leadership mind* that focuses continually on meeting the expectations of constituents and stakeholders.

If you want to find an organization where *good to great* leaders exist, look for situations where extraordinary results exist but where no individual steps forth to claim excess credit. As noted in the chapter on stewardship, each individual must put aside self-interests and personal agendas for the good of the organization. This happens when individual leaders acknowledge their sole purpose is to work together to accomplish that mission—not a minute sooner.

TIME MANAGEMENT

"Control your own time. Don't let it be done for you. If you are working off the in-box that is fed to you, you are probably working on the priority of others."
-Donald H. Rumsfeld

"Nothing else, perhaps, distinguishes effective executives as much as their tender loving care of time."
-Peter Drucker

You might not think you have the time to read this essay. Besides, you might say, a countless number of books, tapes, and seminars exist on the subject if you can just find the time. On Amazon.com, I found 1184 results for books addressing Time Management.

There's no question that time management is a critical leadership skill. And with all due respect to Mick Jagger and the *Rolling Stones*, most of us would not agree that "... time, time, time is on my side ..." We are more likely to side with *The Guess Who* as they lament "No time, no time ... I got, got, got, got no time."

I have drawn most of this discussion about leadership and time management from Peter Drucker's timeless classic,

The Effective Executive. First published in 1966 and only 175 pages, it remains one of the best management guides ever written.

If the ancient philosopher advises an individual to "Know Thyself," Peter Drucker advises the effective executive to "know thy time." Drucker argues that leaders do not first start with tasks; rather "they start with their time ... they start by finding out where their time goes."

Service on the board of directors of a volunteer organization can be very time-consuming. It is not just about meetings, although they can be large devourers of time. If you are truly committed as a board leader, you will find inordinate demands being made on you to attend conferences serve on committees and represent the organization at various events. There are also the not-so-small chores of doing your homework for board meetings, keeping up with pertinent reading, constituent involvement, and fundraising.

When I served on the Eanes school board, we had regularly scheduled meetings only once per month; the truth of the matter is we had specially-called meetings too, as well as sub-committee assignments several times a month. If you have served on a school board or some other volunteer organization, this is old news.

Serving on a board has its own set of special rewards, but unless you are managing your time effectively, you may feel that you are being drawn and quartered by all the competing demands. Consider these five actions:

1. Focus on priorities, value, and results; what critical issues which will yield the most benefit to the organization should the board focus on? Or as Drucker urges, "focus on the results and performance goals of the entire organization."

2. Plan the meeting agenda carefully, stay on track, don't over-schedule, and end on time. Do your homework and be prepared.

3. Identify and eliminate those items and time-wasters that do not need to be done by the board or done at all. Which of the board's activities could be done just as well by somebody else, if not better?" Remember the 11th Commandment: "Thou shalt not micromanage."

4. Learn to say no. More to the point, learn how to say no without feeling guilty. My own experience cautions that you can better serve the organization by not accepting every offer or request that comes your way. Doing so virtually guarantees burnout.

5. Remember the 12th Commandment: "Thou shalt not waste the time of others." Be organized, be prepared, and be conscious of the time demands of others. They will very much appreciate you for it and be inclined to return the favor.

++++++

Volunteer organizations face a multitude of challenges in achieving their missions, from limited resources to unlimited demands. And while money is always a problem, the recruitment of effective volunteers has become the Achilles heel of many organizations.

Why? Once again the answer is time; or more precisely, lack of time among the most wanted volunteers. The organization must understand how the time demands of its volunteer pool changes over time and must be prepared to restructure based on the needs of the *volunteer*—not the organization. This is a collective leadership responsibility of the board, working with the paid staff.

A *Wall Street Journal* article "Giving Time: Volunteerism on the Run," (November 5, 1999) captures the essence of this problem. According to the article, "Volunteerism is experiencing a severe case of commitment phobia. ... The numbers reveal a troubling trend: While a record 109-million people are giving time—14% more than in 1995—they're doling it out in ever-smaller portions. The average volunteer put in 3.5 hours per week last year, down nearly a full hour from three years earlier, according to Independent Sector, a Washington research group. Indeed, if you add up all the time volunteers gave, the total has actually dropped slightly since 1995."

The reasons behind this trend are not all that complicated: families with both spouses working full-time, caregiving for elderly parents, competition with church, school, and community organizations, carpooling, soccer games, and so on. Generational attitudes can also be a factor as the post-boomers and later generations are less inclined to give up significant blocks of their time.

But it is also true that the message being sung loud and clear by virtually all volunteers, generational differences notwithstanding, is "Don't waste our time!"

TIMING

"You've got to know when to hold 'em, know when to fold 'em. Know when to walk away, know when to run ... "

–Kenny Rogers, "The Gambler"

"Timing is (almost) everything. Knowing when to introduce an initiative, when to go before one's constituents – and when to hold off – is a crucial skill."

–Doris Kearns Goodwin

What does timing have to do with Leadership? Everything, Peter Drucker writes, "Exercising leadership is like having sex! Position is important, but timing is everything."

For example, take an election for a school-bond issue. The need for money for a new school, renovation of current facilities, or a new gymnasium may be immediate. But holding the bond election shortly after taxpayers just received notice of increased valuation on their homes, could very well doom the bond passage, no matter how much it is needed or justified. Good ideas put forward at the wrong time have less chance of success than bad ideas at the right time.

Effective leaders know the value of striking while the iron is hot, but also understand that a successful strategy may require laying behind the log until the timing is right. While intuition helps, leaders must constantly stay in tune with their constituents and be aware of what is happening in the world around them. Is the economy booming or in recession? Have current events conspired to create increased cynicism or pessimism among voters, donors, or members? Is church attendance increasing or decreasing because of changing demographics in the community?

It is a key responsibility of board members to follow the trends in business, public affairs, technology, society, economy, and demographics that might affect the organization or community.

✦✦✦✦✦✦

Political campaigns serve as an effective model for understanding the importance of timing. Political campaigns involve stages that build toward Election Day. The timing of political advertising is critical, both in terms of effectively spending money and in keeping the candidacy from peaking too soon.

Managing a political campaign either for a candidate or for other ballot initiatives is both an art and a science. Campaign consultants know they must allocate spending at the proper times to continue to build momentum and develop a positive image for the campaign. They also know they must be prepared to respond to negative ads with exactly the right message at exactly the right time.

Nor are communications and management strategies static. These change from election to election as well as during a single campaign. For example, the introduction of early voting, where the polls are open several weeks before Election Day, means that the campaign cannot wait until the week before the election to advertise heavily. Certain advertising must be timed to coincide with early-voting patterns, particularly in those areas with a history of high early-voting turnout.

It is unfortunate that former President Lyndon Johnson is often remembered only for the failure of the Vietnam War, because he was a political master that accomplished much good for this country. One of his great skills, according to presidential historian Doris Kearns Goodwin, was his "instinctive sense of timing" about when to move forward with a legislative proposal. For example, Johnson introduced the Voting Rights Act following the bloody civil rights march on Selma, Alabama. With the pictures of police attacking unarmed citizens still fresh on their minds, Congress acted under overwhelming pressure.

In real estate, it is "location, location, location." In political campaigns and matters of public policy, the three most important factors are "timing, timing, timing." Board leaders must always keep the issue of timing in mind when making strategic decisions that have major implications for the success of the organization. Timing is a crucial skill of leadership.

TRUST

"A man who doesn't trust himself can never really trust anyone else."
— Cardinal De Retz

"The highest proof of virtue is to possess boundless power without abusing it."
— Thomas Babington

After years of earning the public trust with its humanitarian actions, one decision by the American Red Cross—diverting funds intended for victims of 9/11, to other uses—launched an avalanche of indignation by the American people and cast a long shadow over the organization's credibility and reputation.

Trust is the heart of a nonprofit organization. Difficult to achieve, it can be lost all too quickly as the Red Cross debacle demonstrates. Constituents, members, and donors base their support on the assurance that the organization will do what it says it will do. "The ultimate question," Peter Drucker writes, "is what should this institution hold itself accountable for by way of contribution and results? What should this institution be remembered for?"

There is a valuable lesson in the Red Cross experience for all nonprofits and public-sector boards of directors. Thousands of nonprofits in the United States perform faithfully and admirably for their constituents and members. But it requires more than just doing good—*it requires accountability.*

Volunteers and donors are attracted to nonprofits because they see the opportunity to participate in a mission that is larger than themselves. Dedicated individuals provide the energy that sustains the nonprofit organization. If, however, the organization becomes tainted by scandal or even the perception of wrongdoing, this flow of human commitment can dry up as quickly as a West Texas creek bed after a flash flood.

"Inspiring trust is important for any organization," writes Robert Watson, the recently retired commander of The Salvation Army. "*But it is life-and-death for a nonprofit.* People invest their time and their money in institutions they believe to be honest and effective."

"Integrity," says Watson "has never counted for more. With everybody watching, you'd better be on track to deliver what you promise. You'd better be who you say you are."

"How can I earn the trust of my sales team?" the young salesman asked his mentor. The answer is simple: "Be trustworthy."

✦✦✦✦✦✦

Several years ago, flying home to Austin from Washington, D.C. on American Airlines, my seatmate was an American pilot deadheading into Dallas-Ft. Worth. He was apprehensive about the possibility of an upcoming strike and its impact on the airline. He was low on seniority and obviously worried about his future.

He loved his profession and was distressed that relations between management and the pilots had deteriorated so badly. Comparing his airline to a competitor, Southwest Airlines, he lamented, "We have great management, but no leadership."

Earlier, I talked about Southwest and its colorful former president, Herb Kelleher, in the context of sustaining results by "focusing on individuals ... not titles." Herb was once asked, "Who are your heroes?"

Herb replied without hesitating, "The employees of Southwest are my heroes ... I salute their spirit, boundless energy, immense good will, and burning desire to excel."

Can there be any doubt why Southwest employees trusted Herb Kelleher to act in their best interests? They trusted Herb because he trusted them.

✦✦✦✦✦✦

Kouzes and Posner identified four questions that you can ask yourself as you go about your daily actions:

1. Is my behavior predictable or erratic? If your behavior is confusing, inconsistent, or indecisive, others cannot depend upon you to behave in certain ways under similar circumstances.

2. Do I communicate clearly or carelessly? If you make statements that are inconsistent with your actions, you will not be trusted.

3. Do I treat promises seriously or lightly? In the chapter on credibility, we noted that a major difference between an authentic leader and one who relies solely on his authority is that the former keeps his promises, and with the latter you just never know. If a leader takes his promises too lightly, then so will his followers.

4. Am I forthright or dishonest? If you mislead or lie, people will not trust you nor will they be willing to put themselves on the line for the organization.

Trust is earned; it is not a commodity that can be bought, traded, or bartered. Additionally, trust is engendered by trusting others. By expressing faith and loyalty toward his followers, a leader will be deemed trustworthy as well.

Appendix A

SEVEN ESSENTIAL QUESTIONS

1. Are you getting the results that you want as a board?
2. Is the board working efficiently?
3. Is the board having difficulty resolving issues or developing policy?
4. Does the board have difficulty reaching consensus on key issues?
5. Do the same issues keep coming up meeting after meeting, year after year, without the board being able to come to closure?
6. Does the membership believe (perceptions are equal to reality) that the board/organization is not meeting its needs?
7. Do members feel they are contributing to the final decisions?

Appendix B

Roles & Responsibilities of Volunteer Board Leaders

1. **Establish policy.**

   - Meet the needs of constituents you represent.
   - Address the needs of the public as well.
   - Set policies that guide your organization to run effectively, legally, and ethically.
   - Recognize policy decisions as those that affect the organization as a whole.
   - Establish the framework within which the staff executive can lead and manage.

2. **Establish a partnership with the chief staff executive.**

   - Set guidelines for authority, responsibility, and accountability of the chief staff executive and the board.
   - Provide support.

3.   Nurture a vision.

- Have a *shared* vision, sense of mission, and plan.
- Take the long view; help put difficult decisions into perspective.

4.   Provide direction through strategic planning.

- Stay in touch with your membership and your professional environment.
- Assess strategic implications of critical issues.
- Identify opportunities and threats.

5.   Assure the financial integrity of the organization.

- Tie financial policies to programmatic goals.
- Maintain sound fiscal policy, practices, and controls.
- Assist in developing and approving the budget.
- Delegate implementation and administration.
- Monitor financial outcomes and performance.
- Think long-term, big-picture; not only annual income/expenses.

6.   Participate responsibly.

- Commit the necessary time or step aside.
- Regularly remind yourself of your role as a leader/director.
- Keep politics in perspective.
- Review agenda materials sufficiently prior to meetings.
- Do your homework.
- Keep the board working on board-level matters.
- Employ committees and staff effectively.

- Suggest potential board members and volunteer leaders.

- Follow trends in the profession and other trends in business, public affairs, technology, society, and economics.

- Take special assignments willingly and enthusiastically when asked.

- Bring a sense of humor to the board's deliberations.

- Be a goodwill ambassador for the organization.

- Actively participate in membership recruitment and retention.

- Support the organization's public advocacy

- Attend events and activities, including the annual conference and educational seminars

- Express opinions consistent with your conscience and convictions, but support the majority decisions made by the board.

- Speak for the board or the organization only when authorized to do so.

- Maintain confidentiality of issues discussed in executive decision-making sessions.

- Serve the whole organization, rather than any special interest group or constituency.

- Avoid even the appearance of conflict of interest.

- Disclose any possible conflicts in a timely fashion.

- Commit to continuous improvement

7. **Commit to board leadership as team leadership.**

    - Know the goal.
    - Know your role as a board member.
    - Provide feedback.

- Respect and value diversity.
- Develop trust and fight fair.
- Pitch in to help.
- Know how to solve problems.
- Spread the credit; celebrate.
- Get results.

8.   Evaluate performance at all levels.

- Policy
- Finance
- Staff
- Board
- Organization

Appendix C

ASSESSMENT TOOLS

Diagnosing Your Board

This is a diagnostic tool the Chairman of the Board and the General Manager of a Co-op can use when evaluating the operation of a Co-op Board of Directors. It is not an all-inclusive tool, but will give the Chairman and General Manager a good handle on the strengths and weaknesses of a board.

Meant for internal use only, you may want to include members of the board in the evaluation and then develop a composite of all scores.

- Characteristics of Boards with Superior Performance
- Board Governance Issues
- The Board's Role in Advancing the Vision, Promoting the Mission and Supporting Strategic Change Initiatives
- Key Board Roles and Responsibilities
- The Effective Board-CEO Partnership

Board of Directors Meetings

These work sheets are for your use only. There are no right or wrong answers to the questions and the Chairman and Chief Staff Officer (and possibly board members) will be the only officers grading the results. This is a tool to help you think about your organization.

Assessing Your Board of Directors

For each of the following assessment tools, rate each statement on a scale of: 1 = Strongly Disagree; 2 = Disagree; 3 = No Opinion; 4 = Agree; 5 = Strongly Agree.

Characteristics of Organizations With Superior Performance. Rate your Organization on the Following Criteria:	1	2	3	4	5
(1=Strongly Disagree; 5=Strongly Agree)					
Maintains a long-term awareness of the organization's future (5 plus years)					
Implements a viable mission					
Creates a board leadership vision of its roles and responsibilities					
Develops a strategic plan-monitored and updated frequently (1-3 years)					
Offers competitive compensation package for the CEO and staff					
Maintains an effective partnership between the board and CEO					
A well maintained "leadership pipeline" thatidentifies prospective leaders and future officers for the board					
Applies an effective use of technology					
Exercises effective committee management linked to mission, objectives, and strategies					
Implements up-to-date set of personnel policies, financial policies, and other internal controls					
Provides Distinctive Member Value to Co-op members					
Responds quickly to members (24/7/365)					
Encourages an effective marketing plan					
Is financially sound					
Exercises good decision-making and judgment					
Promotes a positive public and community image					
Provides service to the community - "gives something back"					
Effectively communicates with members					
Sets high performance standards with frequent evaluations					
Is politically involved on behalf of its members					

Board Governance Issues	1	2	3	4	5
(1=Strongly Disagree; 5=Strongly Agree)					
The board does its work efficiently.					
The board has no difficulty resolving issues or developing policy.					
The board doesn't have difficulty reaching consensus on key issues.					
The board is capable of overcoming divisiveness on issues to achieve consensus.					
The board nomination and officer selection-process encourages new leadership to pursue board service.					
The board is committed to improving its own effectiveness.					
Board directors are encouraged to enhance their individual leadership skills.					
There is a formal orientation program for new directors.					
Committee charges are clear and related to the association's strategic plan or specific board action.					
There is a process for handling committees that perform little or no functions but are required by association bylaws.					
Committees and task forces are held accountable by the board for achieving objectives and meeting deadlines.					
The Co-op conducts an annual orientation for committee and task force chairs.					

The Board's Role in Promoting the Mission and Supporting Strategic Change Initiatives:	1	2	3	4	5
(1=Strongly Disagree; 5=Strongly Agree)					
The board understands the long term needs and goals of the Co-op.					
The board communicates the long- and short-term goals to the membership.					
The board maintains an effective strategic planning process, which includes an annual review and evaluation.					
The financial plan is directly linked to the strategic and long-range planning process					
The board focuses on strategic and policy issues rather than operational issues.					
The board commits resources to strategic change initiatives that will add value to association benefits and services.					
The board commits resources to those strategic change initiatives that will address problems that may cause severe penalties for the organization if no action is taken.					

Key Board Roles and Responsibilities	1	2	3	4	5
(1=Strongly Disagree; 5=Strongly Agree)					
Board members know they are accountable to the members for the organization's successful operation.					
The board ensures financial integrity of the organiza-tion, including setting financial policies tied to programmatic goals and maintaining sound fiscal policy, practices, and controls.					
Board members actively identify and encourage-potential board nominees who will serve with distinction and make significant contributions to the work of the board and the Co-op					
Individual directors speak for the board only when authorized to do so.					
Although staff members are employed to serve the board's will, the staff is given latitude to make decisions and is not micromanaged.					
Board members serve the Co-op as a whole, rather than any special interest group or constituency.					
Board members avoid even the appearance of a conflict of interest and disclose any possible conflicts in a timely fashion.					
Directors ask questions, express opinions consistent with their conscience and convictions, butsupport the majority decisions of the board.					

The Effective Board - CEO Partnership	1	2	3	4	5
(1=Strongly Disagree; 5=Strongly Agree)					
The board and CEO agree on the chief executive's performance targets for the coming year.					
There is explicit consensus within the leadership about what constitutes success.					
A process is in place to assess chief executive performance, including feedback to the CEO that identifies performance shortfalls.					
The CEO is measured against the performance targets negotiated a year earlier.					
There is openness and honesty in communication with no hidden agendas.					
It is clear that the CEO receives direction from the board as a whole (or its designee) and not from individual members.					
The CEO has sole authority to direct staff, including hiring and firing.					
Board members consider the CEO a peer.					
The CEO has the latitude to determine the means employed to achieve the ends agreed to, subject to keeping the board informed.					
There is clarity of roles and responsibilities; the board knows the staff's role and the staff has a similar understanding.					
The CEO seeks opportunities to increase the board chair's effectiveness and recognition.					
The CEO is committed to increasing the leadership capacity of the board.					
Although it may be informal, the CEO and board chair have a process that facilitates clear communications and a mutual understanding of roles and responsibilities.					

Board of Directors Meetings	1	2	3	4	5
(1=Strongly Disagree; 5=Strongly Agree)					
The board focuses the majority of its time on strategic issues and policy outcomes rather than organizational concerns, administrative details, and committee reports.					
If surveyed, board members would respond that time spent at board meetings is a productive use of their time.					
Board members are comfortable about expressing their opinions on controversial issues.					

BIBLIOGRAPHY

References and Sources

American Society of Association Executives Foundation, *Facing the Future: A Report on the Major Trends and Issues Affecting Associations.* Washington, D.C.: ASAE Foundation, 1999.

Bennis, Warren, *On Becoming a Leader.* Wilmington, Massachusetts: Addison-Wesley, 1989.

Bennis Warren and Burt Nanus, *Leaders: The Strategies For Taking Charge.* New York: Harper and Row Publishers, 1985.

Bennis, Warren and Patricia Ward Biederman, *Organizing Genius: The Secret of Creative Collaboration.* Reading, Massachusetts: Addison-Wesley Publishing Company, Inc., 1997.

Block, Peter, *Stewardship: Choosing Service Over Self-Interest.* San Francisco: Berrett-Koehler Publishers, Inc., 1993.

Burns, James MacGregor, *Leadership.* New York: Harper and Row, Publishers, 1978.

Drucker, Peter, *The Effective Executive*. New York: Harper and Row, 1966.

Drucker, Peter F., *Managing the Nonprofit Organization: Principles and Practices*. New York: Harper Collins Publishers, 1990.

Freiberg, Kevin and Jackie Freiberg, *Nuts! Southwest Airlines' Crazy Recipe for Business and Personal Success*. Austin, Texas: Bard Press, Inc., 1996.

Gardner, John, *On Leadership*. New York: The Free Press, 1990.

Gergen, David, *Eyewitness to Power: The Essence of Leadership Nixon to Clinton*. New York: Simon and Schuster, 2000

Giuliani, Rudolph W., *Leadership*. New York: Hyperion, 2002.

Greenleaf, Robert K., *Servant Leadership: A Journey into the Nature of Legitimate Power and Greatness*. New York: Paulist Press, 1977

Harvard Business Review on Nonprofits. Boston: Harvard Business School Publishing, 1994.

Handy, Charles, *The Age of Paradox*. Boston: Harvard Business School Press, 1994.

Harari, Oren, *Leadership Secrets of Colin Powell*. New York: McGraw-Hill, 2002.

Hayward, Steven F., *Churchill on Leadership: Executive Success in the Face of Adversity*. Rocklin, California: Prima Publishing, 1997.

Hesselbein, Frances, Marshall Goldsmith, and Richard Beckhard, Editors, *The Organization of the Future*. San Francisco: Jossey-Bass Publishers, 1997.

Hesselbein, Frances and Rob Johnson, Editors, *On Creativity, Innovation, and Renewal*. San Francisco: Jossey-Bass Publishers, 2001.

Hesselbein, Frances and Rob Johnson, *On Leading Change*. San Francisco: Jossey-Bass Publishers, 2002

Hesselbein, Frances, Marshall Goldsmith, and Richard Beckhard. *The Leader of the Future*. San Francisco: Jossey-Bass Publishers, 1996

Hesselbein, Frances, *Hesselbein on Leadership*. San Francisco: Jossey-Bass Publishers, 2002.

Humes, James C., *Churchill: Speaker of the Century*. Briarcliff Manor, New York: Stein and Day/Publishers, 1980.

Humes, James C., *The Ben Franklin Factor: Selling One to One*. New York: William Morrow and Company, Inc., 1992

Kaltman, Al, *Leadership Lessons from Ulysses S. Grant*. Paramus, NJ: Prentice Hall Press, 1998.

Katzenbach, Jon R., *Real Change Leaders: How You Can Create Growth and High Performance at Your Company*. New York: Random House, 1995.

Koestenbaum, Peter, Leadership: *The Inner Side of Greatness*. San Francisco: Jossey-Bass Publishers, 1991

Kotter, John P. and Dan S. Cohen, *Leading Change*. Boston: Harvard Business School Press, 1996.

Kotter, John P., *The Heart of Change: Real-Life Stories of How People Change Their Organizations*. Boston: Harvard Business School Press, 2002.

Kouzes, James M. and Barry Z. Posner, *Credibility: How Leaders Gain and Lose It, Why People Demand It*. San Francisco: Jossey-Bass Publishers, 1993.

Lamb, Brian, *Booknotes: Stories from American History*. New York: Perseus Book Group, 2001.

Leider, Richard J. and David A. Shapiro, *Repacking Your Bags: Lighten Your Load for the Rest of Your Life*. 2002.

Lipman-Blumen, Jean, *The Connective Edge: Leading in an Independent World*. San Francisco: Jossey-Bass Publishers, 1996.

McCauley, Cynthia D., Russ S. Moxley, and Ellen Van Velsor, Editors, *The Center for Creative Leadership: Handbook on Leadership Development*. San Francisco: Jossey-Bass Publishers, 1998.

Mourier & Martin Smith, PhD., *Conquering Organizational Change: How to Succeed Where Most Companies Fail*. Atlanta, CEP Press, 2001

Moxley, Russ S., *Leadership & Spirit: Breathing New Vitality and Energy into Individuals and Organizations*. San Francisco: Jossey-Bass Publishers and The Center for Creative Leadership, 2000)

O' Toole, James, *Leading Change: The Argument For Values-Based Leadership*. San Francisco: Jossey-Bass Publishers, 1995.

Phillips, Donald T. *Lincoln on Leadership: Executive Strategies for Tough Times*. New York: Warner Books, Inc., 1992.

Phillips, Donald T. *The Founding Fathers on Leadership: Classic Teamwork in Changing Times*. New York: Warner Books, Inc., 1997.

Quinn, Robert E., *Deep Change: Discovering the Leader Within*. San Francisco: Jossey-Bass Publishers, 1996

Rosen, Robert H. with Paul B Brown. *Leading People: From the Inside Out*. New York: Penguin Books USA, 1996.

Rosen, Robert H., Patricia Digh, and Marshall Singer, Carl Phillips, *Global Literacies: Lessons on Business Leadership and National Cultures*. New York: Simon & Schuster, 2000.

Snyder, David Pearce and Gregg Edwards, Ph.D., *Future Forces: An Association Executive's Guide to a Decade of Change and Choice*. Washington, D.C.: ASAE Foundation, 1984.

Strock James M., *Reagan on Leadership: Executive Lessons from the Great Communicator*. Rocklin, California: Prima Publishing, 1998.

Watson, Robert A. and Ben Brown, *"The Most Effective Organization in the U.S.": Leadership Secrets of The Salvation Army*. New York: Crown Business, 2001.

Whyte, David, *Crossing the Unknown Sea: Work as a Pilgrimage of Identity*. New York: Riverside Books, 2001.

Williams, Pat. *The Paradox of Power: A Transforming View of Leadership.* New York: Warner Books, 2002.

Zander, Rosamund Stone and Benjamin Zander, *The Art of Possibility: Transforming Professional and Personal Life.* Boston: Harvard Business School Press, 2000.

ABOUT THE AUTHOR

Robert A. Floyd, CAE, President of Strategic Leadership Consultants, has 29 years of achievement in association and nonprofit management, public affairs, and building strategic alliances and communications, strategic planning, effective governance, board leadership training, and organizational performance.

Robert is a Certified Association Executive (CAE) and served as the President and Chief Executive Officer of the Texas Society of Association Executives (TSAE), a 1200-member professional membership society. He received the TSAE Distinguished Executive Award.

Robert served as an officer of the American Society of Association Executives (ASAE). In 1998 he was named an ASAE Fellow.

He also led a major trade association and has lobbied before the Texas Legislature and the United States Congress. He has served on the board of directors of various nonprofit organizations, including the Mental Health Association in Texas and the Texas Association of Nonprofit Organizations (TANO). He also served on the board of directors of the Austin Convention and Visitors Bureau.

He has held elective public office as a two-term school board trustee and on a local water district board.

In November 1995, he was recruited to teach a six-week association management-training program in Zimbabwe, Africa. He administered an examination to establish an international standard for certification.

Robert holds a Bachelors of Arts Degree in Government from Texas State University and a Master of Arts Degree in Political Science from the University of Arizona. He currently teaches Nonprofit and Association Management at St. Edwards University in Austin, Texas, and State and Local Government at Austin Community College. He has published several articles on leadership and non-profit management, and has special interests in the study of leadership, the American Civil War, and politics.

Robert is a native Texan and a 30-year resident of Austin. He served in the U.S. Army and is a Vietnam Veteran.

Strategic Leadership Consultants Web Site:
www.stratleader.com
Robert A. Floyd's Email: robert@stratleader.com